My Six-Year-Old Inner Artist
Everybody has one!

How to live defiantly creative in an increasingly unpredictable world

WENDY WICKHAM FALLON

Cover Art and Book Design: Wendy Wickham Fallon

Front cover photograph: 'Penney Wickham', 1960

by Earle Wickham

Publisher: Night Well Press

Editor: Deborah Kyle

Copyright © 2015 Wendy Fallon.

ISBN: 0986269301
ISBN-13: 978-0-9862693-0-1

Dedication

To my parents, Carol Jean Ward & Bentley Wickham

Contents

Acknowledgements   ix

Introduction: Living in an Unpredictable World   11

Chapter 1: Finding Joy   9

    Making Change Happen 10

    Discovering Joy 10

    Mining Memories 11

    My Biggest Dream 14

    Good Health, Love & Fortune 17

    What Makes You Happy? 19

    Surviving or Thriving? 21

    From Dream to Reality 23

    Positive Universe, Positive Attitude 25

    My Dream Statement 32

Chapter 2: Nurturing Your Dream   33

Identifying Your Inner Artist 34

Definitions 34

Caring for Your Dream................................. 39

Being in Your Right Mind............................. 40

Overcoming Fear 47

Building on What You Do Well 51

Thinking Positively......................... 53

Chapter 3: Survival Surfing   61

Unpredictable Circumstances 62

Riding the Rollercoaster 65

Making Tough Decisions................................ 66

Chapter 4: Investing in Your Passion   71

Making Time for Making Art 72

Your Passion, Your Life, You 74

Balancing Act................................ 75

Chapter 5: Living & Thinking Creatively   81

One Day at a Time 82

Adaptive Creativity 84

Defining Yourself 85

When Enough is not Enough 87

Living in Balance 89

Remember to Have Fun! 90

Chapter 6: Learning New Tricks   93

Organize Your Thoughts 94

Organize Your Time 97

Organize Your Space...................................... 104

Organize Your Life's Work 106

Creative Employment 111

Chapter 7: The Importance of Art   113

The Importance of Art and Community.............. 114

Sharing & Giving Back.................................... 120

To Retire...or not?... 122

Chapter 8: Case Studies for Meaningful Work   123

Defining 'Work' 124

Living Defiantly Creative in an Increasingly Unpredictable World.. 127

Chapter 9: Celebrating the Creative Life   131

Diana Alsip, Artist & Photographer 132

Marian Crane, Mixed Media Artist & Writer 134

Bonnie Lou Coleman, Artist & Musician..................... 136

Laurie Fagen, Visual & Performing Artist, Writer 139

Patricia Hall, Painter 141

Jacque Lynn Keller, Acrylic Painter & Designer 144

Dale Kesel, Photographer... 146

Debbie Kyle, Crochet & Knit Designer 149

Bob Leighton, Photographer 151

Jacqueline Price, Painter 154

Sandra Neumann Wilderman, Painter 157

Appendix A: Play and Learn Exercises   159

Appendix B: Resources & Suggested Reading   161

About the Author   163

Acknowledgements

I would like to thank the following people, without whom I could not have written this book: Diana Alsip, Marian Crane, Bonnie Lou Coleman, Laurie Fagen, Patricia Hall, Jacque Lynn Keller, Dale Kesel, Debbie Kyle, Bob Leighton, Jacqueline Price, Karen Wickham Sharpe, Sandra Neumann Wilderman…and to my two men, Joe Alsip and Tim Fallon for providing their enthusiasm and unflagging support.

WENDY WICKHAM FALLON

Introduction:
Living in an Unpredictable World

This story is not about becoming a traditional artist. It is about discovering the wellspring of creative survival that exists in all of us and allows humans to thrive in an unpredictable world.

Like most Baby Boomers, I grew up in what I feel was the emergence-of-women-from-the-home-and-into-the-workforce era. Mom stayed home and was there for my sister and I at every moment. She provided the perfect example of the 1950's housewife, and Dad was committed to supporting his family. They never argued in front of the kids, and yes, we had a house, two cars, two kids, a cat and a dog.

My parents provided everything we needed, including encouragement for whatever activities we were drawn to and skills we exhibited. I was an artist from the moment I could hold a crayon, with their blessing. I showered them with brightly colored drawings of butterflies, flowers, houses, or anything else that caught my eye.

Twenty-five years later and somewhere in the middle of my own life as a wife and happy-to-stay-at-home mom of three,

I was challenged with the initially overwhelming responsibility of providing a steady income. I was completely unprepared.

I had to find a way to make money, nurture and care for my children, and stay sane; not a rare situation in the larger scheme of things, but devastating all the same.

No one suggested I 'follow my bliss.'[1]

I began to panic as the reality of my situation became apparent. As an artist and dreamer, I found very little practical or emotional support for making a living by making art. Dreaming and 'making art' were generally discouraged and condemned as self-indulgent by the world at large, especially with three small children. And by this time, my parents were gone.

After living on savings and child support for three years, I eventually hit on a solution. I re-packaged a set of my previously unpublished writing skills, taught myself how to use a computer and contemporary software, and eventually found employment as a corporate and technical writer. This more than paid the bills and helped provide enough income for my family to live on comfortably. During this time I also remarried and was now part of a two-income family.

I was proud of myself for taking on the technical world with such success, but there was still that niggling little voice in the back of my mind that could not be ignored.

---

[1] Joseph Campbell, *Pathways to Bliss, Mythology and Personal Transformation* (New World Library; 1ST edition, 2004).

My 6-year-old inner artist was throwing a tantrum.

It wasn't long before I discovered that I hated what I was doing. The effort of suppressing my sometimes messy, freethinking, inner artist was exhausting.

Of course, I didn't expect to feel happy all the time, and I was wise enough at this point to know that euphoria was best experienced as an unexpected treat. But I at least expected to feel some sort of personal fulfillment from working 50 hours a week along with the steady, generous paycheck and benefits. Instead, I felt like a right-brain dominant personality stuck in a nightmare of highly complex data, unrealistic deadlines and frustration. I seemed to be continually stressed, disorganized and easily flustered in a technology-based, highly competitive industry.

Faced with remaining in this high-stress, overly political environment until the end of my days (unless I was laid off, down-sized, right-sized, or any other term you'd like to use for suddenly finding yourself unemployed), I knew I had to make a significant change, if only for my own health. But what was I thinking? I was contemplating walking away from eight years of the highest paying, benefit-rich job I had ever had in my life and an income my family depended on.

It took intensive planning, a change in personal attitude, negotiation with and the education of loved ones, and unshakable determination to change careers. After eight years as a corporate technical resource, I left my high-paying employment to open an art gallery with a friend and business partner in 2007. It was one year before the economy tanked. Believe me when I say there were very few who thought I wasn't crazy, or at the very least, irresponsible.

On the other hand, I began to add vital positive energy back into my life by following my 6-year-old inner artist and making my own art and writing. The personal satisfaction and joy that came with creating my own magic was priceless, and I began to feel much more self-confident.

The first year and a half of Art on Boston Gallery, located in historic downtown Chandler, AZ, marked one of the euphoric high points in my own personal development. My business partner, talented fiber artist and successful entrepreneur, Laurie Fagen, and I made our own art, celebrated the art of others, taught and reveled in art. But in 2008, the recession hit hard in Arizona.

At the time, I saw my life as a series of cycles of varying levels of fortune. Having reached the pinnacle of a dream long pursued, I mistakenly believed that I couldn't sustain it without a cost. Eventually I experienced the fall from that glorious attainment along with all the accompanying financial and personal crises that come with a broken business in a failing economy. I lost the Gallery, my income, peace of mind, financial security, and friendship, and eventually my family's home.

I didn't think I, my family, or my marriage, would survive. I felt guilty for the seeming hubris of following a self-centric dream. In addition to all this, I was at the bottom of the career ladder looking up, at an age when others were contemplating retirement.

In my various work roles as co-owner of an art gallery, artist studios, and classrooms; professional artist and instructor; and technical, corporate and creative writer, I've explored work as both an employee and independent provider in both creative and technical industries. As a direct result of acknowledging my own personal creativity, my life has evolved into a joyous, balanced, fulfilling existence of family, work, and making art.

My Six-Year-Old Inner Artist is for anyone who thinks *I can't* - i.e. can't draw, write, sing, make time for yourself, or move into the future with hope and positive anticipation.

Fear, combined with physical and emotional exhaustion can undermine any dream.

Human resilience and creativity becomes especially important as the Baby Boomer generation ages into the years after midlife. This lengthening span of life has become a new social challenge as many of us reject or simply cannot afford the traditional idea of retirement.

As you read this book you will find discussions about how I began to think outside of the ordinary and changed my life for the better.

My hope is that you will take information and lessons from what I've learned about my own creative journey and how I have survived and thrived, living in an increasingly unpredictable world. Hands-on exercises in the Play and Learn sections in each chapter help you create tools for living a better life. Examples of what you will find:

- Chapter One: re-discover past dreams, childhood wishes, goals or ideas you've lost or abandoned.

- Chapter Two: identify your inner artist and learn to define past dreams, choose what you would like to focus on, and develop options for turning them into reality.

- Chapter Three: learn to apply your inner artist to seeking answers to difficult questions, and how to make tough decisions.

- Chapter Four: pursue, maintain and strengthen your dream.

- Chapter Five: nurture your inner artist, create balance in your life and redefine work and play; learn to re-align or define your priorities.

- Chapter Six: develop personal strategies for using your inner artist to make changes in your life.

- Chapter Seven: learn about the increasing importance of creative thought in all aspects of society and at all ages, along with suggestions for using your inner artist to apply your dream to creative employment.

- Chapter Eight: read about examples of meaningful work and how I re-defined my own work and the lessons I learned in the process.

- Chapter Nine: read about ordinary individuals who have used their own awe-inspiring creativity not only to survive, but to thrive in this world.

My goal in My Six-Year-Old Inner Artist isn't just about telling my own story. It is to provide you with a toolbox with the right mix of inspiration, motivation and practical application to allow you to reach for your highest potential for living and working creatively, and to enjoy a richly rewarding life. It is never too late to make a change. I did.

WENDY WICKHAM FALLON

Chapter 1: Finding Joy

Making Change Happen

I believe that happiness and personal fulfillment are affected by the following things:

- Our thoughts and attitudes.
- Our activities.
- Our environment and the people around us.

You can literally change your life and even your point of view by changing the thoughts you fill your mind with[2], but how?

First, you must find your source of hope. Just as Peter Pan advises Wendy[3] and her brothers that they, too, can fly by thinking the happiest thoughts they can, you can also find joy by unearthing positive thoughts in memories, visual cues, activities, and supportive friends and family.

Discovering Joy

Can you remember any times in your life when you felt joyfully swept away by what you were doing? Do you have any activities in the past or present that have engaged your imagination, piqued your curiosity, made you want to learn more, or simply left you totally and completely overwhelmed with awe or delight? Do you feel too young, old, tired, poor, busy, or disillusioned to take the time and energy to recapture those feelings?

---

[2] Dr. Wayne Dyer, *Change Your Thoughts, Change Your Life* (CA & NY: Hay House: 2007).

[3] J.M. Barrie, *Peter Pan and Wendy* (Hodder & Stoughton, United Kingdom, Charles Scriber's Sons, United States 1911).

Has your logical brain or someone else told you how impractical, selfish or immature your dream is; that you will fail, or that it is a waste of time, simply because they cannot see, share or otherwise experience your vision?

Have you stopped enjoying or participating in pastimes that made you want to dance or sing along, or brought a feeling of enjoyment? Some of my favorite pastimes are browsing through a bookstore on a weekend, listening to music, having an inspiring conversation with another artist, writing or painting anywhere, or spending time with my family. You may be challenged by time or money, or are missing someone in your life who is no longer available to enjoy these activities with you. Finding new paths to joy might start with discovering new places or ways of enjoying past activities, or finding new activities in familiar places.

Mining Memories

As a child I remember being happiest when reading and drawing. The positive feedback I received from my parents and extended family sparked my awareness of my ability to draw and 'make art.' I still remember the magic of reading two of my favorite children's books, both of which I still have, that re-enforced my desire to make art. I unearthed these childhood experiences not long ago to re-examine why I had enjoyed them as a child. They were so significant that they managed to survive moves, purges, yard sales and decades of life. Why?

Harold and the Purple Crayon, by Crockett Johnson[4]

Harold is a little boy who actually redefines his reality with

---

[4] Crocket Johnson, *Harold and the Purple Crayon* (Harper Collins Publishers, 1952).

his artwork.

He is able to draw his way into and out of his imagination at will and deal efficiently with the childhood dilemma of being small and powerless. My 6-year old self found that amazing, magical purple crayon truly impressive. As an adult, I still feel a powerful and astonishing magic associated with being able to draw. How easily adults lose that feeling of wonder! I know now that childhood delight, unbound curiosity and the unquestioning belief in the magic of simple beauty and nature is a blessing. Any adult who can revive those feelings of unfettered joy in everyday life is rare.

The Wish-Tree, by John Ciardi[5]

In John Ciardi's *The Wish-Tree*, a small boy learns to take responsibility for and to nurture his wish to receive a puppy for his birthday. The night before his big day, his father gives him the word "TAKECAREOFYOURWISH"; telling him he will need to learn what it means before he can have a pet. As he goes to sleep, the boy dreams of meeting a very sad, floppy dog made from rags who explains he is a forgotten wish. I can still remember how the illustrations in this book fired my imagination. The loose, simply-drawn black and white drawings created by Louis S. Glanzman presented a dynamic, magical world reached through a small door in the trunk of a oversized tree.

Although the story is intended to teach responsibility for one's choices, my mind was much more impressed with the idea of combining drawing, magic and unlimited possibilities.

---

[5] John Ciardi, *The Wish-Tree* (Crowell-Collier Press, 1962).

As I re-read this story, I also realized that perhaps forgotten wishes held a clue to what my adult self really wanted in this life.

Play & Learn: Remembering Joy

Everyone has a back-story; events, objects and individuals that significantly affected you during childhood and early life to create the person you are now. Here are a few questions to consider.

Use a large sketchbook with a sturdy front and back cover. This will be your Dream Journal. You will utilize this tool throughout the exercises in this book for discovering personal truths and cultivating your dreams. Record your answers in your Journal.

1. Did you have a favorite holiday, vacation location, book, movie, friend, or any other object that you particularly enjoyed or related to?

   For instance: I still dream about my grandparent's shore house, where I spent every summer of my first 15 years. Why? I've since realized it was a magical place of sea breezes, sand, salt water, strange and amazing sea creatures, and piles of pine cones. It was a safe, secure environment in which my imagination ran wild with more freedom than I had at home. I could be anything or anyone I wanted.

2. Did you have anything in the past that was so significant that you still have some remnant of it in your current life?

3. Did any of these things create a dream for the future or a now-forgotten wish?

4. Go through your list of items, and record why you feel they were so significant to your younger self.

My Biggest Dream

Daydreaming seems to have been one of my favorite re-occurring past-times.

I remember sitting in class, doodling and day-dreaming my way through math or science in high school, neither of which were my favorite subject. Drawing, dreaming and reading helped me survive the teenage angst, acne, awkward social moments, and intensely shy, painful self-awareness I suffered through. Instead of cheerleading, choir, or band, I hid out in the Art Room. I passed my free periods hunched over a desk or table with my fingers covered in paint, clay or graphite, completely lost in whatever the current art project was, and dreaming about creating art for the rest of my life.

I've been carrying this dream ever since. It is difficult for me to imagine anyone unable to dream, imagine or otherwise think beyond a personally uncomfortable or depressing existence. Having a vision gives me a goal to move towards, a future worth working for and meaningful activities.

Dreams and imagination are, after all, what move our society into the future. These are the tools humans use to create and manifest new technology, medical breakthroughs, and solutions to overpopulation, disease, ignorance, hunger, poverty, and many of the afflictions of our world. Having a vision of a better life in impoverished, depressed parts of the world may even mean the difference between life and death.

I believe everyone has the potential to create hope and dreams in their lives, and ultimately a happier existence. Daydreaming gives your inner artist a place in which to consider the question "What if?" I highly recommend daydreaming in moderate quantities for anyone stuck in the minutia of everyday stress.

The first step towards making a change in your life is being able to imagine that change. Imagination is the human ability to problem-solve through challenges that threaten our survival. Perhaps it is what also makes us human.

Play & Learn: ME Diagrams

1. Spend some time dreaming and imagining your vision. What sort of future would you feel passionate and intensely happy to pursue, regardless of money or acknowledgment? Don't be afraid to create the biggest dream you can imagine and write down every detail and word as it comes to you.

   Try thinking about dreams you might have had in high school, but were perhaps too shy or afraid to share. Maybe you believed they would never happen. And remember, there aren't any right or wrong answers or self-judgment in this exercise.

2. Open to a clean page in your Dream Journal. Draw a circle in the middle of a page and write the word 'ME' in the middle of it. What color would your spirit be in a perfect world? Shades of gentle blues, cool greens, passionate reds, oranges or yellows? My favorite color is a combination of orange and pink. Using crayons, color pencils, markers or any medium of your choice fill in your 'ME' circle. Don't worry about 'staying within the lines.'

3. You may have trouble imagining what color you'd like

to be in the future and may only be aware of how you feel right now. You may be angry, tense or frustrated and your 'ME' circle might be slashes of dark red, black, and bruising purple. Don't be afraid to simply go with how you feel in that moment.

After you've finished reading this book and completed all of the exercises, try this first activity again and see if your colors have changed.

4. For every activity or topic you enjoy or would like to learn more about (past, present or future), draw a separate circle and place a word or two of description inside it. Arrange these additional, smaller orbs around your 'ME' circle.

5. If you have identified a passion, activity or dream you return to over and over throughout your life, link that circle to your 'ME' circle with a bold line. Begin to make notes around this favorite pastime or idea. List every single idea you can think of to add it into your life. (Examples: take a class, dedicate a space in your home for it, read about it, look it up on the Internet).

    Chances are that if it is something you enjoy, you are most likely good at it and can count it as one of your strengths. Remember the foremost criteria in choosing a dream is that you find it fulfilling, easy and enjoyable. Think positively.

6. Paste magazine photos, drawings, texture and color swatches around your notes that represent your idea of the perfect space, location or time of day in which this activity might look like in a perfect world. Pick any personal or magazine photos, or illustrations that

remind you of how that activity makes you feel.

7. Choose 2 or 3 other circled activities, in order of preference, and repeat steps 4 and 5 for each one. Use as many pages as you need.

Your goal is to build a list of the activities you are attracted to and enjoy, and the ambiance of your preferred living and work environments.

Do you want your living space completely separate from your work area? Do want them combined?

Do you feel you need a studio separate from the space in which you pay the bills? Can you pursue this activity from your kitchen table or garage? Which of these imaginings would you like to see become reality? These are just some of the questions you may find answers to during this exercise. Have you designated a space for daydreaming and inspiration?

Good Health, Love & Fortune

I am now in the second half of my life. Why should I suddenly become so aware of how happy or fulfilled I am? This self-awareness was a burden during my earlier years, because really, there wasn't anything I could do about it, right? The choices I made because of the pressure from others and my own lack of general knowledge and self-confidence sent me down the paths I was destined to travel for the rest of my life.

This acceptance of destiny was re-enforced by the words of a trusted high school instructor who told me that the more choices I made, the fewer I had left. What a weight of responsibility to burden a young adult with!

By the age of 20 there were no more free play times, and as always, no day-dreaming, no 'rocking the boat' of social expectation; I was an adult and I had accepted a life filled with anxiety from pursuing the *right choices*.

I married my high school sweetheart and was mostly happy for the next 20 years. I completely ignored that infernal niggling little voice that was by now just a desperate whisper in a dark corner of my mind.

Each of us defines happiness differently based on events and circumstances, past and present in our lives. Generally speaking, the feeling of happiness could depend on a combination of factors, and not just a single item.

The formula that works best for me has evolved into the following:

Good Health + Good Love + Good Fortune = Happiness

Taken at face value it might seem too simplistic and general to do any good, like those tiny strips of placating words found inside a fortune cookie. But it is the result of years of the distillation and refinement of my own collection of memories, experiences, education and relationships.

Although this book does not address the study of 'Good Health,' I cannot stress enough how important it is to take care of your physical self. Your world will simply run much smoother if you can fit in the exercise, nutrition and good habits needed to keep your body in the best shape possible.

How would you define your happiness formula? What does happiness have to do with living triumphantly through the good times and the bad? Sometimes just a slightly unsettled, indeterminate feeling is the only hint that life could be better.

> Trust and listen to your intuition. It is the voice of your inner artist crying out for recognition! (And yes, you DO have one.)

What Makes You Happy?

Happiness can be that euphoric feeling that makes you smile, laugh, feel satisfied, fulfilled, or uplifted. It can be elusive for some, overflowing for others, and its source is unique to each and every one of us. Some identify happiness with one or more activities and drawing has always been one of mine. Identifying a source of happiness can establish a direction in life. How do we find it?

Journal Entry: Beginning Drawing for Those Who Think They Can't

Today was class day, and my first and only student had arrived early, nervously smiling at me as she introduced herself.

In her late 50's, finishing up a successful career, with her children out on their own, she looked tired and adrift. Her face was etched with nervous fatigue. As we got to know each other during the beginning of class, she admitted it had been a long time since she'd done anything for herself.

She had signed up for the 3-hour class over the phone, her voice filled with a mix of trepidation and hope.

"I don't have a creative bone in my body – I can't even

draw a straight line. I never had the time to learn but I've always wanted to," she explained in embarrassment. "It wasn't something I was encouraged to learn...but then I guess you hear this all the time!"

The class title was self-explanatory.

"'Beginning Drawing, for Adults Who Think They Can't.' That would be me!" She laughed.

I carefully guided her through the drawing process; patiently showing her how to pull or push the pencil across the paper. At the end of the third hour she looked down at her work in astonishment. What she saw was a simple rendering of a pleasing arrangement of three shiny, round apples of differing sizes. "I can't believe I did this!" she exclaimed, her voice reverent and a bit awe-struck.

It is this very instant of self awareness, the moment in which my students suddenly realize that they've actually created something as mystical and magical as 'art,' that makes my spirit and my heart resonate with happiness.

Can you think of a time in the past when you felt a euphoric feeling of satisfaction, which made your heart resonate with happiness? If you have experienced it in the past, you can reach that feeling again.

For my students these could be the first steps towards seeking out the things in their lives that make them feel euphoric; things that make their own hearts sing. These moments could lead to a new attitude and a life to be joy-filled and happy about.

> If you think you aren't creative enough to make art and you make something so beautiful that it astonishes you, what else can you do that you didn't think you could?

Learning to draw is a wonderful way to start building the confidence you need to move towards your dream, but certainly not the only one.

It definitely served to bolster my own self-confidence and feeling of identity as a teenager and throughout my life, but there are as many paths to happiness and feelings of fulfilling abundance as there are humans. Learning something new, like photography, painting, a second language or even how to read and write can spark the same self-confidence.

Overcoming fear and discovering and developing your strengths are just the beginning.

> The simple act of defying the words "I can't" is powerful indeed and making art can increase your creativity and actually change the way you see and think.

Surviving or Thriving?

It has always angered me that creative work doesn't seem to be compensated in our society to the same extent as technical work.

I believe that in the work arena, left-brain functions are rewarded with higher income. In other words, technology pays, and art does not. Why does work have to be tough, exhausting, or unfulfilling? Why can't work be play, or at least creative?

Why shouldn't I be able to make a living doing what I am best at and enjoy most? Remember, the math, science and technology taught in school were never among my favorite subjects.

I've also wondered why I've taken so long to finally focus my life on my own positive creative energy. One of my younger struggles was with the feeling that I didn't deserve to be happy or creative, that somehow I needed permission to actually pursue my own happiness.

After all, tradition often preached hard work, the importance of raising my children and taking care of my house and husband. And I did. I followed all of the unwritten rules, buried my inner artist and put all of my energy into becoming the very best mom and wife on the planet.

Late in my 30's I awoke to the realization of my own, irretrievably broken marriage.

My parents were gone; I had no job, no income of my own, no advanced education and three small children. But one of the most devastating realizations was the fact that I hadn't created any art in more than a decade, and in attempting to return to drawing, I found I couldn't do it. My muse and my gift had all but disappeared. Had my inner artist died from neglect?

Perhaps if I had paid a bit more attention earlier on to that little voice in the back of my mind, I wouldn't have found myself in the very pit of despair and depression. In this instant I knew I had to take responsibility for my own life, and the lives of my children. So I finally began to listen to my intuition, my inner creative, that tiny breath of God.

There were no other choices left.

What I have learned over the ensuing years about the world and myself continues to astonish me.

From Dream to Reality

My own experience of using art to conquer my fears and move forward towards the dreams in my life also enabled my journey from frustrated, cubicle corporate employee towards a fulfilling life as an artist and writer. I moved away from feeling cornered and was able to identify and choose from among the opportunities I'd unearthed and been presented with along the way.

I must point out, however, that because each of us is unique, your detailed path to fulfillment will differ from mine. Keep in mind that although it takes hard work and perseverance, a happier, more fulfilling life is possible.

Today I count many accomplishments as evidence of my inner artist at work: co-owner of a contemporary art gallery, artist studios, and classrooms in the Phoenix metropolitan area; gallery manager, contributing and professional artist, art teacher, and writer.

I have patrons and collectors of my artwork throughout the U.S, with a few in Canada and Europe. I've been published as a writer and an artist. As an unforeseen by-product of my creative pursuit, I now have a job that I do well and enjoy. I've accomplished much more in my life than I'd ever expected to by listening to this tiny inner voice.

By identifying and accessing your inner artist you will begin to think positively, change your attitude and thoughts, and build your self-confidence.

I can still remember very clearly a point in my life when I made the conscious decision to pursue creative play over technical work.

I left my first corporate employment in 2005, despite the fact it meant a lack of benefits and money.

Journal Entry: A Changed Point of View

Oh my God! I can't believe I surrendered my badge, the magic key to a fortified commercial building the size of a warehouse. I spent 8 years in that building and more waking hours sitting in a cube than I spent with my family.

And I just exited my employment, threw in the towel, and gave up. Why do I feel such a mix of emotions?

I should be celebrating! This is what I wanted, right? I've spent the last three years planning for this very moment on this very day; the day I'd leave and not return. I should feel elated, liberated and free, but today all I could feel were waves of heat radiating off the pavement in the parking lot, through the soles of my shoes and into my face, and an overwhelming fear of the unknown.

This job might have been the best paying, benefit-laden employment I'll ever have and I have so many friends here. How could I throw this all away?

My slip of composure seems to undermine everything I've been working towards. I feel like I've jumped off the edge with no safety net, free falling, and for what?

I can't live without money!

I'd like to believe I'm moving towards creative freedom. I've determined to chart my own employment and use my own skills, talents and inner artist to create an income. I've read every book about self-employment and talked extensively to entrepreneurs. I've written my business plan, set up my office/studio, set aside money and plunged off the cliff.

When I climbed into my car it occurred to me that if I were to ask anyone about what I had just done, the consensus of popular opinion would be one of overwhelming condemnation.

I also realized with a rush of pure bliss that I wouldn't be fighting the traffic in the morning to return to a job that was literally shortening my life with stress.

Positive Universe, Positive Attitude

I'm not particularly religious, but I am spiritual. In pursuit of my dreams for myself, my family, friends and others, I practice prayer. I consider prayer to be positive energy, and firmly believe my prayers are always answered. Many times I've not seen or recognized the answers until time has passed, and the answers may not be those I've expected. Often the results have left me breathless with the realization that I have been heard.

I have expanded this practice to include the theory that if I present positive energy to the world in everyday activities and to the people around me and take positive steps of action to push forward in a desired direction in my life, the world will respond to me in positive ways. Opportunities, although not always the ones I envision, will present themselves.

Being open to all possibilities will ensure I don't miss them. I often wonder how many I've missed because I wasn't paying attention.

The magic of this idea is that sometimes the Universe hands me opportunities and answers I've wished, prayed, and yearned for, but cynically, or perhaps realistically, not expected.

> I firmly believe that if you can picture your goal(s) in your mind, then you can also make them happen.

Here a few examples from my own life.

At the age of 24, while living in North Cape May, N.J., I began designing my own patterns for and creating stained glass boxes with hinged lids embellished with seashells. I started selling them through a local gift shop in Cape May, and during art shows along the boardwalk.

I remember thinking how exciting it would be to have my own gift shop and stock it with all artist-made artwork and handcrafts. I actually recorded this thought in a list of future goals and thought of it over several years. I didn't really expect it to happen.

As life continued, I gave up stained glass because of the lead content in the solder. I went on to have and raise three children, divorce and re-marry, move from the East Coast to Arizona, and in 2007 became the co-owner of Art on Boston, a gallery in which all merchandise was artist-made.

Another example might be my corporate career, which blossomed as a simple wish to hold a job with benefits. After my divorce I was wrestling with the lack of income and medical coverage. I had never held a job for a large company, and knew I'd never make enough in retail to help support my family.

When I landed my first professional job, it was literally the answer to a prayer and what I considered to be a true miracle.

The pinnacle of dream-into-reality, however, was the creation of an idea for a multi-purpose art gallery with a friend and former business partner.

The visualization and drawing of floor plans, discussions of location, colors, and floor finishes were immensely exciting, but absolutely nothing compared to the overwhelming reality and awe of entering the completed Gallery for the first time.

Journal Entry: A Beautiful Space

I saw the completed Gallery today and it was so exciting!

With the 17-foot high, original molded tin ceiling and 3,000 square feet, it's the most beautiful space I've ever seen. The front of it is walled by sliding-glass doors and unusual 60-year-old pressed glass tiles that provide indirect sunlight. It is a bright and inviting venue in which to display artwork and teach. With two spacious, enclosed classrooms and a kitchen, it will give us a place to teach, hold exhibit openings, or even to rent out for receptions or private parties.

We have so many plans, and several artists have

already signed up to exhibit and make art! What really blows me away is that it truly exists – created from two-dimensional notes, doodles, to-do lists, meetings, license applications, and floor plans. Our baby, our dream, is now a reality, an actual building. Now what do we do?!

Forming a partnership with the Universe has always been one of my favorite philosophies. This is not a new idea, but an important one. I trust that God and the Universe 'have my back.'

Working through my challenges, opening myself to as many possibilities and solutions as I can think of, and sending positive thoughts and actions out into the world in the form of resumes, dream journals, free writing, future goals, prayers, or art has not only helped me find answers, but fulfillment.

When you feel you need permission to seek out your own happiness, trust in the Universe and listen to your intuition. Somewhere along the way, I've learned to listen to that little voice inside, my own intuition and inner artist, and it now tells me over and over that I deserve my own happiness. Not only is it possible to reach and live my dreams, but I deserve to live life abundantly and deeply.

You, too, deserve to be happy.

> Learn to trust yourself and the Universe that made you and celebrate your life! You are worth it!

Play & Learn: How Happy Are You?

A. You may not be aware of anything amiss in your life but the feeling of a gentle discontent or you may be at a point in your life where you feel something must change or you'll simply cease to exist. Consider the following statements below:

1. I feel angry because I followed all the 'rules' throughout my life and I've lost my retirement, my security, my job, and/or my loved ones.

2. I've lost my faith in God and people.

3. I'm too uneducated, too inexperienced, too young, too old, too poor, too helpless, too tired, too (fill in your own words) to start over, change my point of view, learn new skills, or think outside the norm.

4. I have a home, loved ones and all the money I've ever wanted and I can count numerous good things in my life, but still I feel unfulfilled, sad, unhappy, (fill in the blank).

5. I feel guilty about feeling unfulfilled, sad, unhappy, (fill in the blank).

6. I don't feel deserving of anything better in my life. After all, there are those much worse off than I am.

7. I feel I need permission to be happy.

8.   Nothing in my life excites me anymore. I have nothing to look forward to.

9.   I feel betrayed by the economy, my friends, my spouse, God, or (fill in the blank).

I am not talking about a feeling of depression so deep you can't see your way out of it. If you feel so sad or angry that you are having thoughts of harming yourself or others, call 911 or call 1-800-273-TALK (8255) for the National Suicide Prevention Lifeline. Search the Internet for a phone number near you and get help immediately. Clinical depression is a serious illness that CAN BE TREATED.

Living in a constant state of euphoria is also unrealistic, if not downright unhealthy. My goal has always been to live a life of emotional balance.

I am talking about the feeling of being forced into a corner and needing something to be excited about, to look forward to, to do something you love.

Perhaps life intervened and you've detoured to have children, support your family, or were put off by well-meaning individuals who discouraged what they felt was an unprofitable career path. I'm talking about those of you who are experiencing an undefined feeling of frustration or helplessness.

If any of these statements reflect or come close to how you feel, read on for additional tools and ideas for defining what you want, how to get there and ways of nurturing those dreams.

B. Answer the following questions. You are your own best friend, and if you sit quietly and listen to your heart, the answers will come. Part of finding the right answer to anything is asking the right question.

1. What would you like more of? Time (with your family, to finish projects, to make more art), financial and/or physical security, fulfillment, space, inner peace, (fill in the blank)?

2. What would you like less of? Stress, anxiety, commuting, clutter, bills, (fill in the blank)?

3. What comes to you most easily? What subjects were your favorites in school?

4. What do you have the most trouble with? Time management, talking with your spouse, public speaking, paying the bills, getting up in the morning, (fill in the blank)?

5. What have you always wanted to do with your time? To work from home, spend more time with your family, make a difference in the world, teach, fly, write, or (fill in the blank)?

6. If you feel the need to solve any one of the challenges facing society today, what would it be?

7. What did you enjoy as a child? Who or what did you want to be when you grew up?

8. Do you remember any childhood books, movies or heroes that you found fascinating? Why?

9.   If you could click your fingers and make everything perfect in your life, what changes would you make?

C. Writing down your dreams and goals is one of the first steps you can take towards turning them into reality. Complete the following as if it were already accomplished. This will set the expectation in your mind that not only is it possible, but that you deserve it.

My Dream Statement

I. _____ am a(n)_____
     (your name)   (writer, artist, pilot, sand painter, etc)

and am _____
(writing, painting, contributing time, living green, etc)

to help/solve _____. I would like have more
          (poverty, starvation, my own problems, etc)

_____ and less _____in my life.
(peace, health, etc)   (stress, anxiety, illness, etc.)

Example

I, Wendy Fallon, am an artist and writer and am making art and writing to help others experience the natural beauty around them. I would like to have more joy, time for my family, financial security and less stress in my life.

Save your Dream Statement. I will explain in a future chapter how to use it to further develop your dream into reality.

Chapter 2: Nurturing Your Dream

Identifying Your Inner Artist

Aside from discovering and nurturing your life's dream, or at least identifying what you would like more of in your life, how do you go about finding your inner artist and why is it important?

I believe identifying your inner artist is simply a way to prove to yourself that you are, indeed, a creative being. In my case, recognizing the fact that I was a creative personality bolstered my self-confidence and cemented my determination to design my own life.

My theory is that every human born with a healthy brain has direct access to both right and left sets of brain functions. I believe that 'making art' uses right-brain resources, which strengthens creativity and creative thought, which in turn improves issue resolution and problem solving.

Definitions

In this book I use many of the common words associated with creativity, however my definitions may be more expansive than you've been taught to expect. I've listed them here to help you understand that each word can be interpreted differently depending on your past education, life experience and personal essence.

Inner Artist

Noun - The creative part of each of us that encourages new ideas, new attitudes, new activities, a new approach to life, and when necessary, survival; imagination.

I did not identify my six-year-old-inner-artist until I was 37. No, she isn't an imaginary friend or the voice of mental illness.

At the time, my inner artist manifested itself in the creative writing and art I began to make in response to increasing stress, anger, fear and depression triggered by divorce and the death of a loved one. It was also at that point in my life when I began evolving from a reactive victim into a proactive survivor.

I now visualize my inner artist as a child of six because that is the age at which I recall my first memories of drawing, coloring and painting. It also coincides with my first challenge in life, that of severe illness. These memories are the origin of my life path.

Since each of us is unique, your inner artist, or creative alter ego, will manifest itself in a vision, skill or talent unique to you alone. I believe everyone has the ability to identify and strengthen this creative part of themselves.

Play & Learn: Finding Your Beginning

Can you find the origin of your own life path? I discovered that my six-year-old self enjoyed playing dress up, looking at and reading books, baking, drawing, or anything at which I was allowed to make a mess. The activity was always more important than the finished product. Making messes gradually morphed into making art.

Often the beginning of your life path can be seen in your earliest memories or photos of yourself.

1. Try to unearth your earliest memories. How young were you?

2. Try to find photos of you as a child. What did you like to do? How and what did you like to play?

Did you enjoy being a leader or part of a team?

3.   Why have these memories stayed with you?

4.   Can you relate these earliest memories to something in your current life?

Art

Noun - New ideas, thoughts, technology, or written, visual and performing self-expression. Anything you do well that you've contributed a portion of your soul or unique essence or point of view to.

Verb – 'is', to be, to exist. 'Our Father Who art in heaven....' (Is it merely coincidence that the act of making art is also that which means to exist?)

Artist

Noun - One who lives and thinks creatively from their own unique essence or being; one who creates or manifests a thought, idea, thing, or vision into reality. One who has mastered a creative skill.

Is an *artist* only someone who makes their living selling their artwork, exhibiting in galleries and museums, or who has a list of patrons and collectors for their work? Does being an artist have anything to do with making money? My answer is *no*.

My own evolution includes the belief that to be an artist is to express myself through making my art; to think and live creatively, regardless of a lack of support, payment or fame. By expanding my ability to think creatively to solve my life's challenges I've taken the initiative to design my own life.

This larger definition of being an artist on a personal and global level encourages me to carve the necessary time out of my life to make my own art and encourage others to find their own joy.

Being an artist is an entire way of life, a way of thinking, and an approach to existence. I now know that my own definition of being an artist includes communicating from my heart, and evolving from the inside out. I cannot just play the part of an artist on the outside; I have to feel, think and live it.

Creativity

Noun - The ability to see, think, live or manifest a vision, an idea, a solution to a problem, a new product or service, or a piece of written, visual, performing or any other self expression.

Verb – To create; to manifest, bring into existence or to make.
I disagree with the popular belief that creativity is associated only with manifesting something that fulfills a need or a necessity, solves a problem and is recognized by society as having done so.

For me *creativity* is any personal self-expression, whatever form it takes, even if you are the only one who sees it.

Success

The definition of success is highly personal. Every individual defines their sense of success differently based on their own criteria or goal: stable finances, meaningful work, the ability to maintain a living space or a relationship, pay the bills, reaching a comfortable retirement, or some other criteria.

I will speak more about defining your own *success* in a later chapter.

Miracle

You will notice that I use this term rather loosely. My personal definition of a *miracle* is any positive or timely event that I cannot explain.

While the formal definition of *miracle* includes documented events that religious authorities can see but not explain, my use of the word signifies anything within my own experience.

I firmly believe in miracles as the source of unexpected, unexplainable joy. Without miracles there would be no hope, and without hope, humanity would not be motivated to look beyond the obvious. I firmly believe in a Power greater than humanity.

Right-Brain, Left-Brain

Although the physical location referenced by the terms *right-brain* or *right hemisphere*, or *left-brain* or *left hemisphere*, has been proven not be the actual right or left physical parts of the human brain, they do denote separate sets of functions.

Typically, the right-brain or hemisphere refers to a creative, intuitive, big-picture, conceptual and project point of view or way of thinking. The left-brain or hemisphere is a much more detailed, analytical, organized, task and time oriented way of thinking.

Using a mix of both right- and left-brain functions is seen as the best approach for problem solving and generally living a balanced life. There is a certain portion of humans, however, who are right or left-brain dominant.

Caring for Your Dream

Once you determine your dream, how does your inner artist help keep it alive?

I didn't realize until my late 30's that in fact, my inner artist popped up whenever I was in crisis. Once I was aware of this, I began to consciously seek her out by focusing on my writing and art.

This happened whenever my dream needed bolstering or I needed to address an issue.

In general, I've nursed my dream of being an artist all my life; adding and subtracting, fine tuning, rearranging the bits and pieces of my plans in my head, and writing out my imaginary dream life. Art and writing have always kept me sane, giving my brain time to rest and recuperate from emotional or physical trauma. Keeping my dream alive serves as a balm to periods of unexpected strife.

After living through 1992, the worst year of my life during which my dad suddenly died and my husband and I separated, I started drawing, painting and writing again. I carved out time for these activities during my children's naptimes, while they were at school, and after they were in bed. I began to make art with them and enjoyed framing and hanging their work. I went back to school to study Architecture.

As I recovered from emotional devastation I slowly rediscovered my love for making things with my hands that I so treasured as a child. That precious childhood experience of being in the moment began to return, and I began to rediscover my six-year-old inner artist.

Now, later in my life as a technical writer with my children grown, I still experience that flame of rebellion that continues to demand that I make art.

Although my time as a corporate employee in the past had always brought much-needed additional income, the experience also created a higher level of stress.

On the other hand, those jobs were miracles in a tough economy during the highest rate of unemployment in the history of the country.

My answer to this dilemma has always been to carve out additional creative time on the weekends and evenings. I survived in those previous corporate positions by devoting as much spare time as possible to exploration, making art, reading and writing, and spending time with my family.

Being in Your Right Mind

I firmly believe that everyone has an inner artist, a creative component that acts as a guide through the confusion and vagaries that come with modern life. Some call it intuition, the Holy Ghost, or guidance from God. Whatever you name it, it is critical to survival. So where do you find your inner artist? I believe it resides in your own right-brain functions.

It is well within your grasp to learn to think and create positive thoughts, manifest a change in your point of view, and motivate yourself to move outside your comfort zones. The popular theory of left-brain and right-brain differences has been expanded to include the idea that both functional sets work together for the best results. Strengthening either the creative or the analytical skill set should encourage optimal brain use.

Using more of your right-brain functions can not only increase your creativity, but may also increase the strength of your overall brain function and problem-solving skills.

How do you think of new ideas and discover new opportunities? The number of visitors to the Gallery who told me they felt 'totally uncreative' amazed me. So many seemed to be suffering from lost income, lost jobs, lost retirement, lost marriages, homes, and peace of mind. How could making art help turn lives around?

I wondered if my students might start thinking and seeing the world with a more positive, altered point of view by learning to integrate more right-brain activities.

Those of you living in Western society may not have been encouraged by the people around you in your past or childhood to pursue the development of right-brain dominant creative careers.

As young children you were most likely curious, creative, and unapologetically candid by nature. This incredibly enthusiastic creativity, however, is usually lost by a young age, mostly through exposure to our educational system and societal discipline. So adding any amount of right-brain creativity in adulthood to the typically dominant left-brain day-to-day analytical experience may help you access additional creative potential.

This increased experience of imagination might manifest as wisdom, intuition, flashes of insight, or creativity. It might often be that undefined 'gut feeling' that helps you solve problems and successfully navigate your life.

I firmly believe that regardless of religion or personal philosophy, all humans born with a healthy brain are given a creative component.

It is your survival tool, giving you access to your essence, spirit, or intuition. Making art requires us to directly access our right-brain functions, and doing so can strengthen our perception of the world around us.

Making art is only one of many ways to accomplish this, but it is also one of the most personal forms of self-expression there is. Your art, your own self-expression, cannot be anything other than an authentic part of you.

> Making art in any form is an expression of what makes each of us unique, and every human has the potential to manifest it.

There are several books explaining *how* to do what artists do (drawing, painting, sculpting, etc.), but very few about how making art, or accessing direct right-brain functionality, *feels*. This is partially due to the fact that we are each unique and experience the process of making art differently. Educators have long known the differences in learning styles based on left and right-brain functional dominance.

Here are just a few of the qualities attributed to left and right-brain functions.

Left-brain	**Right-brain**
Detail Oriented, Specific	Conceptual, Holistic
Logical, Factual	Intuitive
Analytical, Structured	Relative
Time oriented	Project oriented
Critical, quantitative	Visual

There are published exercises that will teach you how to move from the left-brain functions to the right. [6] Those of you who are able to pursue and enjoy a creative pastime have already made this leap sub-consciously.

Understanding the elements of composition, color, line, texture, music and thinking in colors and pictures comes to you more easily than to your left-brain-dominant counterparts.

Left-brain functions, on the other hand, keep you organized and focused on details, but possibly not as innovative as you'd like to be. The best approach includes a mix of both right and left functions.

For the left-brain, analytical, highly organized personality, the simple act of learning how to draw, therefore, opens up whole new vistas of possibilities. Drawing causes you to truly see the world around you and can briefly quiet the left-brain habit of analysis and often-critical internal chatter.

Drawing, or any other activity of creative self expression, is not only an excellent way to practice directly accessing your right-brain thinking, but is also one way to distract your mind from everyday stress and anxiety.

> Your right-brain skill set can become the source of your intuition and imagination.

Just as deep sleep, meditation and prayer are known to be therapeutic for a healthy, stress-reduced life, so too is

---

[6] Betty Edwards, *Drawing on the Right Side of the Brain* (Jeremy P. Tarcher/Putnam, a member of Penguin Putnam, Inc. 1999).

spending time in your creative zone accessed by the right hemisphere functions of your brain. When you are in *the zone*, you are unaware of time, your surroundings or your body. You relax, and your breathing becomes light and even. You have no awareness of time or space. Being in the zone gives your analytical, left-brain a chance to turn off and rest.

If I don't carve enough creative time out of my life I experience higher levels of stress. The following entry was written during my first eight-year career as a corporate employee.

Journal Entry: A Right-brained Artist in a Left-brained Job

I feel so out of control!

I know I should be more organized and efficient to work effectively, but in a corporate environment it seems that time is literally money, and money seems more important than humanity. So I've been trying to maintain an attitude of 'adaptive creativity.'

I've managed to develop my previous strengths (i.e. my 'creative writing' has become 'technical writing') into tools that make me valuable in any department. It's challenging to be so detail oriented and work fast at something that is so technical and opposite to painting and drawing! It is especially difficult to stay on task and meet aggressive deadlines when my 6-year-old inner artist wants nothing better than to throw tantrums and scribble wildly on the walls.

As I improve at my job, I'm trying to make time for my art. I do manage to get out of bed early enough every morning to visit the local coffee shop and write, draw, and paint for 30 minutes before work. Pouring my heart out into an illustrated manuscript every morning makes the remaining 9 hours of technical work bearable.

I seem have it all; a regular, generous paycheck and benefits, and my artwork on the side.

I've met many artists who are now retired from a lifetime career of whatever paid the bills, with a stable retirement income and seemingly all the time in the world to pursue their art.

It's a viable path, but it isn't one I want right now.

I don't feel like a 'real' artist and I'm not even sure what a 'real' artist is! It's taken me four years to adjust to having what feels like a split personality. I pretend to be a detail oriented perfectionist during the day, and collapse after work at home too exhausted to make art or even think clearly. It's getting harder to get out of bed in the morning.

Play & Learn: Thinking from Your Right-brain

A popular statement among artists is 'to draw what you see, not what you know.'

This statement refers to allowing your eyes, hands and right-brain functions to take charge, and forcing your left-brain know-it-all to fall silent.

Moving from your left-brain to your right can be accomplished through a variety of exercises.

45

The following activity is popular with many drawing instructors and banishes feelings of time and space. If you practice this, meditate or exercise regularly, you'll find yourself in the zone. Thinking from your right-brain can be refreshing, restful and encourage creative thought.

1. Pop your favorite corn, grab a drink and settle down with a blank page in your journal. If you don't have any popcorn, crumple up a piece of blank paper.

2. Taking a pencil in one hand, and a plump, robust piece of popped corn or crumpled wad of paper in the other, turn in your seat until you can no longer see the drawing page or your pencil.

3. Set a timer for 20 to 30 minutes. The longer you take, the more beneficial the exercise.

4. Without looking at the page or lifting your pencil, focus your attention on the lines that define the nooks, crannies and outlines of your piece of popcorn or crumpled paper, and move your pencil to draw those lines.

As this exercise progresses, your logical left-brain will try to interrupt your focus with such thoughts as:

"This isn't something I recognize! I can't understand these squiggles you're making! I don't recognize them as numbers, letters, or any kind of symbol I've ever seen before!"

Or,

"This is SUCH a waste of time! What am I supposed to be learning? These lines don't look like anything!"

You may begin to feel frustrated or even anxious, but if you ignore these thoughts and continue with the exercise, you will find your left-brain giving up entirely, and your right-brain taking over. You will begin to feel relaxed and *in the zone* where the passage of time and sense of effort diminish. Your mind holds nothing else but the lines you are following with your eyes. This is your creative zone.

It is accessed through your right-brain functions and with practice, you will be able to make the jump from left to right-brain thought processes more readily.

I find this especially useful when waiting in long lines or sitting in traffic for long periods of time. I begin to notice the lines, textures and colors around me, which often provide the basis for a new painting.

It is in this zone that your inner, continuous and often negative commentator falls silent and you begin to experience a sense of peace. And it is in these quiet moments your hidden muse and your potential for innovative thoughts, solutions or art is at its highest. This is where your inner artist resides.

Overcoming Fear

Failure

Overcoming the fear of failure depends on your definition of success.

Taking one step towards your dream in the form of a class,

47

or one hour spent at your desired activity, or even telling someone about your goals, is a beginning. But how do you define success? Is it simply taking that first step? I say *yes*! However, your ultimate goal is to persevere, to return to it over and over until it becomes part of the fabric of your existence. And to do this, you have to believe, or at least hope and dream, it can be achieved. You cannot be afraid to try.

I firmly believe that there are no accidents and all experiences and education are valuable. Listen to your heart, your intuition, and write down what you'd really like to be doing, or how or where you would like to live, work or play. That first step could be the beginning of a new life.

Do not listen to greed or fear. Be specific about what it is you are striving for.

I keep a journal of ideas, thoughts and visions and try to write down everything that passes through my head having to do with my making art and writing. Very often they take the form of drawings and doodles.

> One of the first steps to reaching a balanced life is to define what it is you are looking for.

What is it you most want to become, do or acquire?

For me this first step required that I truly knew what I considered being an *artist* meant, on all levels of my being. I had to learn more about myself. There were many times when I felt like a housewife and 'wannabe' artist masquerading as a technical writer.

I realized that if I did not value myself as an artist, neither would my co-workers, friends and family. To attain my dream, I had to believe that it was possible.

Change

Some of you may identify your goal as complete inner peace with no creative movement forward; simply existing with no finance, relationship, health or emotional issues to worry about. I, too, have had the urge to 'be a tree;' to live without any demands on my existence or time. I believe, however, that humans are by nature creative beings and that to stop evolving on any level can be self-destructive.

> Change is a part of life; it is inevitable, for good or bad, and just as time never stops, neither does change. Why not determine a portion of the change in your life and choose your own goals?

To continue to evolve is to move forward, learn and live. The Universe, your personal environment, and life itself are never static. At the very least we all must adapt to the changing world around us, and our inner artist can guide us.

The only failure in life is to not take that first step, ask that first question, take that first class, and to stop moving forward.

Criticism & Rejection

The next step is to take action. Many emerging, as well as established, artists are afraid of rejection.

Fear can keep you from moving forward. Some artists take the criticism of their work very personally because on some level of consciousness they realize that their work comes from the most private and treasured part of themselves.

Chronic criticism in any form can create a feeling of rejection and decreased self-worth, culminating in a paralyzing fear of self-expression.

Criticism can come from an internal or external source. As if we didn't have enough critical review from often well-meaning individuals, we also have a built-in critical voice of our own. Creative personalities are famous for being their own worst critics, often listening to their own left-brain critical analysis to the detriment of their work.

As I've become more confident as an artist, I've been able to place more and more of my artwork in the public realm and learn to take the criticism lightly; to pick and choose which suggestions make sense to me and which don't. Sometimes I ignore critical comments altogether! I try to remember that most good critics aren't criticizing me as a person.

Just as every artist's work comes from a unique place, so does a viewer's emotional reaction to art.

Success

During my life my own fears have included that of success. Every time I reached a goal, I would celebrate briefly and then realize my success had brought with it additional responsibility that I wasn't confident I could handle. I was afraid.

It took me several years to understand that because of this fear, I was sabotaging my own efforts to make art. When I realized this, I made the decision to make art several times a week wherever I was; in public, in the Gallery, and regardless of viewer's comments.

Eventually, each of these pieces of artwork sold to the patron who had the deepest emotional reaction to it. Somehow I was touching the hearts of my collectors and establishing a brief moment in which they could relate to me on an emotional level. This was a good start to building my self-confidence and abolishing my fear of success.

> Moving toward your dream requires physical action and overcoming the inertia of the familiar, often placing you outside of your comfort zone.

Building on What You Do Well

Knowing what you do well and your own style of learning goes a long way towards making good life choices. Focusing on the tasks you excel at builds confidence, and knowing what environment you work well in is a plus. My strengths are learning and working well in a project-oriented rather than a detailed-hourly-oriented environment.

I learn best visually and if I can draw or imagine a picture of new information, I will remember it. What do you consider your strengths and weaknesses? Here are some of mine.

Anyone who has stood in front of a large audience to give a speech or presentation understands the nervous anticipation that can range from mere butterflies to outright nausea prior to going on-stage. I suffered, and still do occasionally, from the latter. By allowing myself to present from my passion for art, I've learned to overcome my stage fright.

Stage fright is one among many of my failings. But it is also one that I overcame through the Gallery.

51

I was so passionate about what our Gallery could provide for those looking for higher levels of creativity that I forgot my shyness. I greeted each person that came through the door with encouragement and enthusiasm, both of which can be contagious. Our sales didn't just feed the bottom line, but the lives and spirit of everyone who took home a piece of artwork or participated in a creative class. This is just one example of taking one of my fears and overcoming it by approaching it from one of my most vigorous areas of knowledge: my passion for sharing art in all its forms.

I believe that weaknesses are not flaws or failings, but proof of our unique, one-of-kind personal essence.

Every human is a unique creation on the part of God, and He treasures each and every one of us. Being as unique as each snowflake or blade of grass is to be celebrated, not condemned.

Build your self-confidence on what you are attracted to and do well. Trust yourself!

Play & Learn: Finding Strength

I'm not going to ask you to list all of your self-perceived faults or failings. Too many of us are overly critical of ourselves, especially when our left-brain is given the opportunity to run wild and cut us down to size.

1. Instead, think about tasks in your daily life, either at work or home, that you dislike or make you feel stressed.

   Can you exchange this activity with someone else for one of their activities that they dislike? Can you hire someone to do this activity? Example: If you own your own business, but don't feel confident about or downright hate doing the bookkeeping, perhaps you can hire a bookkeeper and spend your time finding new business leads instead.

2. Establish or search for a barter group in your area. Search for 'Barter' on the Internet, and find local groups and countrywide associations that will tell you how to trade for goods and services, both on an individual as well as business level.

3. Sometimes learning more about the activity you dislike may bring such a feeling of accomplishment and self-satisfaction that you'll discover it isn't as dull, time-consuming, or mind-numbing as you first believed. For instance, up until I returned to college as an adult to study Architecture, I never considered myself technically inclined. I hoped my art skills for design presentation would carry me through my studies.

   I was amazed to find the study of construction methods to be particularly interesting, and there are few courses more technical in the study of architecture.

   In recent years, I've discovered I also have an aptitude for software applications, something I wouldn't have known if I hadn't given myself an opportunity to learn different software applications.

4. Search for easier alternatives, new software or read about a process that may save you time and money in these activities.

Thinking Positively

Many of us fall victim to our own negative inner voice.

This is the insistent, on-going commentary in your head that loves to throw roadblocks into your path. Mine said:

"You're not a real artist! You'll never earn enough money to keep your home, pay the bills, and survive, much less thrive. Haven't you learned by now that you must commit totally to your left-brain technical skills to get the big bucks?!"

Your inner critic can create so much negativity that it may take a fair amount of courage to defy it. Remember that the negative energy it spouts is not always the truth.

Why not make art, or write, or sing, or carve wood, or…(fill in the blank)? Why not take that first step towards simply enjoying the process of learning something new? There's nothing wrong with taking a few minutes, or hours, for something that makes you feel joyful.

I used to be a worrier. Look at all the trouble I used to have standing in front of an audience. My feeling of panic was the direct result of listening to my negative voice spout about what *might* happen.

I tell myself now that it is a waste of emotional energy. If I've done the very best I can to prepare, then why waste the energy and time ruining perfectly good hours before the event? Worrying about the unknown or uncontrollable doesn't change anything but does create additional stress and can possibly make you ill, or at least ruin your experience.

Based on the concept that positive begets positive, and negative begets negative, the idea of positive thought has been explored and written about by a number of authors.

If you don't think you can do it, why bother?

> If 'to exist' is positive and 'not to exist' is negative, doesn't the very fact that you exist demonstrate the triumph of positive over negative? Therefore you are meant to be here!

Internal Support

There are several ways to get around negative thinking. By practicing positive thoughts, you can actually push the negativity out of your mind. Prayer, mantras, affirmations, and visualization can all be used to accomplish this.

Journal Entry: Emptying My Pockets

I can't sleep. I've been trying for hours. Tim is snoring, and I'm thinking about taking my pillow and moving down to the guest room.

My brain just keeps going around and around; money, work, moving house, the holiday's coming up, and no time to write, no place to paint. It's a constant stream of negative thought. If I don't get up and do something I'm going to scream!

I get up and wander into the kitchen for a drink of water, and look at the moonlight out on the patio. I can hear the rustle of bedclothes as Tim rolls over and stops snoring.

I return to bed, laying on my back, and start breathing deeply and slowly. As I inhale into my stomach I picture a brilliant white and sparkling light I call 'God's breath' flowing into my skull.

As I allow the breath to escape through my barely opened lips, I relax all of my muscles as completely as possible from the top of my head to the tips of my toes. I envision all the stress flowing from my body.

After a few minutes, I isolate my worries, one by one. I picture each worry as a rock in my pocket, weighing me down, making me feel sad and heavy. I visualize taking each rock, one at a time and placing it into a cardboard box. When I've emptied my pockets, I fold the flaps on the top of the box closed, pick it up and hand it up into the shining light above and all around me. And I say, "I trust You to take care of these for me."

I'm not aware of falling asleep until my alarm goes off the next morning.

Play & Learn: Meditation

Several meditative methods can help you alleviate negativity, and relax your body and mind.

1. Search the Internet for local classes or general information for gentle yoga. This type of yoga combines meditation, breathing and stretching and grants you an increase in positive energy and flexibility. Find a class nearby, or purchase a DVD to learn from at home.

2. Investigate Tai Chi Chuan. There are simplified versions of this meditation through movement and is often shown in the media being practiced by groups of Chinese residents in city parks.

This meditation originated in China as a martial art. There are classes and DVDs from which you can learn.

3. Dr. Wayne Dyer has written several great books for meditation. Visit your bookstore, Amazon.com, or search the Internet for 'Dr. Wayne Dyer meditation'. My personal favorite is a small, slender book with a DVD titled *Getting in the Gap: Making Conscious Contact with God through Meditation.*7

Play & Learn: Affirmations

An effective tool in banishing negativity and bolstering a positive attitude is to fill your mind with positive words. These words can be used as an affirmative statement.

Return to the Dream Statement you wrote in Chapter One. This is an excellent paragraph to use as an affirmation. Write it out in your Dream Journal several times a day.

Distribute it on post-it notes in places where you will see it everyday, i.e. the bathroom mirror, the front of the refrigerator, or on the back of your front door so you'll see it as you leave for work each day. Read it, write it or memorize and repeat it before you go to bed at night. Make it the last thing at night and the first thing you think about in the morning.

Your mind will begin to accept the statement as true and inevitable. Your subconscious will direct your actions and

---

7 Dr. Wayne Dyer, *Getting in the Gap*. (Hay House, CA & NY, 2003.)

thoughts until you take the steps necessary to make it reality. You can have more than one affirmation. You might have different ones for short-term and long-term goals. Some affirmations can be very short, but still amazingly effective. My simplest affirmation is: "I am an artist and writer."

External Support

Another way to circumvent negativity is to surround yourself with a supportive network; friends who encourage you, applaud your success, and can be happy for you.

Why subject yourself to someone who poses as a friend but in reality is jealous or unsupportive of your goals? A rare synergy swirled throughout our Gallery among the many artists who visited or worked there; a creative, positive energy that enabled both my business partner and I to remain excited about our own art, the Gallery, and the artists who shared it with us.

How can you use a positive attitude to affect those around you or to change your environment?

Journal Entry: Ripples in a Pond

I went to the pharmacy today to pick up my meds, one of which had been called in by my doctor for a minor infection detected during an appointment an hour before.

When I arrived I was thrilled to find there were only two others in line in front of me.

When my turn came, however, I was told my prescription had not been filled yet and if I would just take a seat it would only be a twenty-minute wait. OK...I could handle this.

Twenty minutes turned into an hour as the line at the counter grew to a dozen or so customers. Two more customers joined me in the row of chairs to await their own as yet un-filled prescriptions. No one gave up their place in line, and those of us seated watched as each of those in line retrieved their pharmaceuticals before us. Finally, my order was ready and the pharmacist called me to the front of line.

"Busy night?" I asked, trying to be sympathetic. "I don't know how you stay so calm."

"Every minute of every day and every night." The gentleman behind the counter answered with a smile. As he bagged my prescription and efficiently stapled the receipt to the outside, he leaned towards me.

"As long as I have a smile," he confided. I must have looked puzzled. "If I smile, my customers smile. If I frown, my customers frown. I can't help the long lines, but I can still make them smile."

This gentleman knew that smiling and a positive attitude were contagious.

Play & Learn: Finding Positive Support

1. Make a list of 5 activities, skills or strengths you enjoy doing, make you feel good about yourself, would like to do more of, or otherwise make you feel joyful.

2. Make a list of 2 or more people you can rely on to support your dream unconditionally. Write down their names and contact information in your Dream Journal.

Call and explain your goals and ask them if they would serve on your personal Board of Directors. Any time you feel discouraged, tired or otherwise find it challenging to move ahead, call someone on your list and ask for positive feedback. Think of concrete, specific questions to ask them or tell them about the latest developments and ask their opinion.

Remember, THINK POSITIVELY.

3. Try smiling more. Smile at someone at work, and see if they smile back.

Chapter 3: Survival Surfing

Unpredictable Circumstances

Life has its ups and downs. Sometimes life can become a series of emotional, financial, and physical crises. In my own experience, these periods of travail have lasted from a few months, to as long as a year or more. Luckily, I've only had two long-term episodes in my adult life, which I feel have been the very worst in my entire time on this Earth. The recent Great Recession was one of them. Looking for creative options became the key to my very survival.

I call changing my thoughts, attitude or circumstances *adaptive creativity*, or *survival surfing*, and it requires me to be mentally flexible and 'roll with the punches.' How do you do this when life throws you a serious curve?

Have you been faced with a loss of employment, potential financial ruin, or a traumatic event from which it seemed impossible to recover? Did you panic, seek help or start brainstorming? Were you able to take control of your situation, act on it and move forward, or did you allow it to defeat you?

For those of you who have devoted your working lives to a corporate job, or any life-long career, losing your employment to the recent recession may have been an emotional and financial disaster. If you are without a job, retiring, looking for employment or a new life that you can enjoy, it can be a challenge to break out of your comfort zone, a life-long routine, or deepening despair.

Finding work may even be impossible. Coming to this crossroad in your life may require you to question everything you've ever believed about yourself and your place or purpose in the universe.

But it may also be the perfect opportunity to try something new.

In 2008, while working at the Gallery, I began to realize that my husband, Tim, and I were sliding into an abyss of debt from which we would never recover.

I had to admit that personal creativity aside, the Gallery wasn't paying our bills and I would be forced to seek out a job that paid enough to do so.

The evening on which Tim and I had the final conversation about it was devastating.

Journal Entry: Detour

Tonight was awful.

Tim called me just after I got to the Gallery.

"I've looked at the bank account, and we're not going to be able to pay the mortgage next month. We've used up the savings, the 401K, and we just can't take any more equity out of the house. You've got to get a real job!"

Tim's voice was high and tight with stress and emotion.

"But I made over a $1,000 this month at the Gallery...!" I could hear my voice trembling.

"I know, Sweetie, but it's just not enough," his voice cracked. "We'll lose the house if you don't. I want you to give up the Gallery and find a steady paycheck.

It's the only way we'll survive."

I knew he was right. Visions of living on the street were a constant reminder. But how could I give up my dream, the goal I'd worked towards all my life?

How could I let my business partner down...leave her running the Gallery single-handedly...not to mention all the money we owed on the business...!

"Wendy, I mean it, this is killing me...I'm not sure I can take any more." A chill went up my spine and my heart froze. Any more WHAT?! Debt? Stress? Anxiety? Fear of the unknown? What would happen if I said no?

I was afraid to find out.

I realized our finances were beginning to erode our relationship, as well as our health.

I knew he was right. If we started missing payments and the bank foreclosed on us, who knew how bad it would get? When faced with the impossible choice between the Gallery and my family, I knew I'd have to go back to corporate employment.

I put my head down on the table in the empty classroom Laurie and I had designed and built, and cried.

I had left corporate employment and technology behind in 2005 to open the Gallery, and in 2008 I returned to it with a heavy heart. I had the training and the experience and my heart gave me no choice but to help support our family.

If I hadn't done so, I believe I would have lost the man in my life I so dearly loved. And how could I put my children at risk? I landed a job on my second interview. Again, this was another answer to yet another prayer.

Riding the Rollercoaster

The Gallery closed in April 2010. By 2011, Tim and I had lost our house, and in 2012 I found myself without a job. Where was my inner artist now; my survival gene? Why couldn't I have a creative job that paid the bills? At that point we knew the national and possibly the global economy was much worse than anyone would admit.

How could I possibly nurture my marriage, my family and my dream through the worst economic recession in recent memory?

Anyone who has lost a job, for whatever reason, may experience it as a slap in the face, a loss of self-confidence, or even feelings of being obsolete and irrelevant.

Because many individuals build their self-confidence around their jobs, the loss of employment can directly impact their self-worth, plunging them into panic, anxiety or depression.

> Don't let ANYONE make you feel worthless or obsolete! You are a uniquely designed human with a one-of-a-kind combination of life experiences and skills.

Tim and I discussed and researched as many options as we could think of and finally came up with a plan. We agreed we had to change our approach to using money, and possibly our entire way of life. And in my heart, I knew I had to become much more creative about finding work I was good at and still earn what we needed. It was incredibly difficult, but just having a plan made us both feel hopeful.

Sometimes just working out a path through the chaos, with whatever help you are able to find, will give you the hope to continue brainstorming. Use your inner artist to imagine new possibilities for yourself and your family.

Making Tough Decisions

In the interest of complete disclosure, Tim and I made the decision to claim bankruptcy.

We first had to come to terms with our own negative attitude about taking such a step. It was a long, hard decision, but we realized that we simply didn't have enough time left in our lives to pay off the debt accumulated as a direct result of the recession and ill health.

That said, I am not advocating claiming bankruptcy. Overcoming challenges creatively, however, may mean entertaining all possible solutions, including those you feel uncomfortable with.

You may be required to learn more about options you might not have considered previously.

I am not an expert on U.S. bankruptcy law, but claiming bankruptcy is a legal option open to residents in the United States. It isn't a decision to be taken lightly or without weighing all the options. It can mean foreclosure on your home (although not always), loss of any equity, and a loss of savings and credit. It does grant forgiveness of debt if you meet the strict criteria.

Greece is an example of a country during the Great Recession where losing everything did not absolve personal debt. Individuals lost their jobs, their savings, and their homes, but were still responsible for paying back their loans. How does one do this?

We finally became convinced that it was our best path when I had to take a detour in January 2011, to the closest hospital, with severe chest pains. I was diagnosed with two blood clots, one in each lung. My physician told me 95% of patients with the same condition did not survive. I spent a week in the hospital, and the resulting medical bills were added to our exploding debt balance.

Once we'd made the decision and contacted a lawyer to help us with the bankruptcy process, we downsized in every way. The bank foreclosed on our home.

Financially, we now pay for everything with cash, and are saving towards a not-so-distant part-time retirement. We have one pre-paid credit card, which is designed to re-build our credit. We stick to a strict budget, and record all expenses and income on an Excel spreadsheet. Tim and I do this together, once a week.

During the process of downsizing we discovered we could live on one paycheck.

Our relocation cut Tim's commute to work in half. Our level of stress dropped considerably. We've grown closer, more resilient as a couple, and very nurturing of each other. And I still have a corner I call my studio, under a window with natural light where I've placed my drawing table.

Events like this tend to redefine your priorities and force you into different routines.

Take advantage of these times to try establishing better practices and habits. How do you react to events that seem beyond your control? Do you become angry or emotional? Try tapping into your inner artist before you make any decisions or give up in despair. Learn about and evaluate all of your options.

Play & Learn: Finding Faith, Hope and Trust

My mother used to tell me events usually worked out for the best. It took me a long time to realize she was talking about faith, hope and trust. Somewhere along the way I began to learn that she was right.

Having faith, or trusting all things to come right in the end is sometimes impossible to believe.

Have you ever been in a situation you could not control in which you felt like it must be the end of world, as you know it?

- Where did you turn for reassurance? God, family members, friends?

- Many turn to religion. What if you've chosen not to be a member of an organized religion?

  Without having a discussion about the pro's and con's of organized religion, I'd like to offer the idea that regardless of religious affiliation, each of you have a creative component. It is this creative component that is your inner artist. Strengthening this part of you will also strengthen your confidence in overcoming any situation.

Once I realized we were not going to be living on the street and were going to survive, I began to feel cautiously optimistic about finding a new direction and employment. It had to be one that combined my artistic skill and education, somehow contributed to society and our retirement, and helped pay the bills.

I once again turned to my inner artist for inspiration.

My corporate *un*-employment gave me time each day to draw, paint, and write, along with searching the online job postings. I started a blog, began posting a Daily Sketch and chose one drawing a week to paint and re-post. I was back to making art and as an added bonus, I was establishing an online presence.

Yes, eventually I did return to corporate work, but not at all in the manner I expected.

WENDY WICKHAM FALLON

Chapter 4: Investing in Your Passion

Making Time for Making Art

Let's say you've identified your favorite creative activity; you now know what direction you want to move in and you've committed yourself to pursuing your joy.

How important is your time management? If you don't earn an income at something you love, you need to make time for nurturing your dreams and your passion. Even if you are earning an income at something you are passionate about, you still need to make time to recharge your mental and emotional batteries.

It has been observed that a constant diet of work is not good for one's health. For example, in Japan it is possible to work oneself to death. It is known as *karoshi.* The Japanese government recognizes the danger of such a workaholic trend and is striving to end it.

Karoshi may represent the extreme of the workaholic mind set, but it demonstrates the human need for creative play and what is now considered leisure. I would take it even further and say all humans need to recharge their mental and spiritual resources by making time for activities that relax and nurture, or otherwise make them feel happy.

This is a tall order for some. There are those among us who are driven to be working or doing something they consider constructive every waking moment. They feel to do otherwise is simply wasting time, or more truthfully they simply do not know how to relax.

When Dad retired from a career of accounting, his sense of

self-worth compelled him to carry around a small pad and pen in his breast pocket. He used these to make lists of things that required his attention. He crossed them off as he completed them, which gave him a sense of accomplishment.

After Mom died he felt he hadn't spent enough time sitting quietly together with her, sharing sunsets over the water, watching the birds, or laughing over simple snippets of humor. He confided to me that he realized he needed to re-learn the act of sitting still to see more sunsets, more wildlife and more of what was beautiful around him. He had to learn the art of *doing nothing*. In his mind, he meant doing nothing constructive.

Dad's solution was to purchase a small boat, and motor around the inlets along the shores of the Metedeconk River in New Jersey. He had spent his childhood hunting squirrels and fishing with his father, skating in the winter, and swimming in the summer. He again returned to spending periods of time outside and away from his to-do list.

I, too, have learned to balance my time between work and play. As a corporate employee, although I now enjoy my work, I consciously schedule creative time and activities into my weekends, holidays and during vacation trips to the beach. I've found that if I don't, work becomes stressful and overwhelming. I am thrilled to now have balance in my life.

Even if you are already earning an income at what you do well and what you enjoy or are passionate about, taking time away from it will keep it from becoming drudgery. Balancing work and play gives your inner artist something to celebrate!

> Each of us has our own optimal balance between work and play. Defining these two components is critical to well being.

Your Passion, Your Life, You

How can a dream turn into reality? There are many steps in this process about which several books have been written. One of the most important lessons I learned in the Gallery was patrons will pay money to own a piece of artwork if they believe in the artist.

It has been said that if you want to sell your product, you must first *sell yourself.* Although an unfortunate choice of words, what does this really mean? In the Gallery I would welcome visitors with a short introduction and tour of the exhibits, studios and classrooms. It wasn't until I introduced myself as co-owner and specifically an artist that I would see a spark of interest. They always wanted to see my artwork, as if being able to match my face to my art somehow made it more valuable…which, in fact, it did.

The artists in our Gallery developed a fan base of collectors who were proud to be able to let others know they had met and were on a first-name basis with the artist whose work they'd purchased. Having a greater number of artists on hand to greet visitors to the opening of a new exhibit usually coincided with a greater number of pieces of artwork purchased.

This has been observed in other retail industries as well. My mother once told me that if she'd ever done direct sales it would have to be something she believed in. In other words, buyers relate to the level of passion in the seller.

The more the seller believes in a product, the easier it is to sell. This is especially true in the creative arts because the product contains an authentic part of the artist. Buyers and humans in general are attracted to authenticity.

If you are lucky enough to make an income with a product or service you are passionate about, you may be more successful. You will become the face, the spirit, the representative of your entire business. You will become your business and you will become an integral part of your product.

> To believe in your product or your business, you must first believe in yourself.

Balancing Act

Each of us will have a different definition of work. Some of us may feel that work is whatever activity generates an income. I believe that few of us feel we have the luxury of choosing to work at what we are passionate about. Many of us work at something we don't enjoy, but feel we don't have a choice. The living expenses must be paid one way or another.

I doubt my Dad worried about whether or not his chosen profession, accounting, was something he was passionate about. If he suffered from the stress of commuting everyday, of the responsibility to provide for our family, or even from physical or mental exhaustion, I was oblivious to it.

It was only later, during conversations with him after Mom died that I realized how proud he was of what he'd accomplished during his working life. He was proud of earning a Bachelor's Degree that in turn allowed him to support his family well.

He measured his success in wealth earned and accumulated, but what he was really proud of was the fact that he'd successfully dedicated his life to providing for his family. His work was an act of love.

My father, however, died at the relatively young age of 67. Would he have lived a longer, and possibly happier, life if he had chosen to work at an activity he enjoyed?

Committing yourself to bringing into existence a family and providing them with food, shelter, education and medical care is no small thing and is to be applauded.

If you can combine it with the pursuit of a personal interest, or grant yourself a tiny slice of time to immerse yourself in something that makes you joyful, you will have even more to offer your family.

Benefits may include improved mental and physical health, higher emotional stamina to deal with family crises, additional income, and an increase in your feeling of well-being.

> Balancing your life by carving out time for your own creativity can grant you increased energy and reduced stress, and benefit your loved ones.

Play & Learn: Finding ME Time

Carving out a regular chunk of time devoted exclusively to yourself might be a difficult step, but is definitely possible. First, you must believe you deserve it. Secondly, you need enough time to truly relax and lose yourself in it, and third, you must have the commitment to pursue your goal. The benefits to the rest of your life include a renewed sense of accomplishment, an increase in positive energy, and a more joyful attitude.

1. Are you the mother of small children? Perhaps you can agree with your husband or partner to trade off caring for the little ones. You might negotiate one evening a week for each of you in which you are free to choose an activity, while the other keeps an eye on your offspring.

2. Are you a single parent? Trade childcare duties with another single parent. This not only gives you precious alone time, but also provides important opportunities for interacting with others in the same situation.

3. How do you find ME time if you are the only wage earner in the household without causing feelings of resentment in your partner? You may be working overtime and your partner may be corralled with the children 24/7. Talk to each other. Communicate your needs and be open to your partner's needs.

    No matter how you do it, seek your partner's buy-in, the pay-off being that you both gain a bit of ME time to indulge in an activity that makes you each feel renewed with positive energy. Invest this positive energy back into your relationship and hire a babysitter for a night out together.

4. If you're alone or without a partner or children, it should be incredibly easy to find the time to indulge in your dream...right? It may be harder than you think. Many of you are in the familiar routine of work, eat and sleep. If you have an extra moment, you clean out a drawer, catch up on laundry, play a video game or watch TV.

Even with my husband's buy-in to pursue my art and writing, I realized I was spending up to 6 hours a day watching TV. We finally worked out a solution, which indulged Tim's TV time and our need to spend interactive time with each other by watching the news together every night.

We discuss what we watch, stay aware of local and global events, and snuggle on the sofa. I also watch less TV. I now rearrange my time so I have time to work on my art and writing each evening and on the weekends.

5. Once you've decided on your goal, set aside a place where you will pursue it. A physical location can be a well-lighted corner with an armchair, an extra bedroom that becomes your studio, or a corner of the kitchen table.

In my own case, my studio tends move around the house depending on the type of project I'm working on. I do have a formal dining room where my drawing table, shelves with reference books and color objects, and some art supplies reside. I also have an empty bedroom where I can set up a portable table and close the door on piles of vacuum cleaner clogging bits and pieces.

6. Provide yourself with a minimum of 30 minutes. Any less will not allow you to relax enough to attain your creative zone. As you learn more about yourself and your dream, you may be able to add additional time over the course of a week. Personally, I try to spend ten hours a week on my own art and writing outside of my day job.

Make this activity a routine.

7. Try to return to the same location to pursue your dream on a regular basis. The strength of your commitment will determine your success. After a time you will notice it has become interwoven into all aspects of your life. You will live and breath it, and with patience, your dream will become reality.

WENDY WICKHAM FALLON

Chapter 5: Living & Thinking Creatively

One Day at a Time

I have discovered that creating balance in my life can also be applied to my point of view. Do I live in the past, present or future, or in a combination of all three? While I believe it is important to have dreams for the future, it is also important that I remember to live in the present.

Journal Entry: Creating New Memories

I spent last week with my sister, Karen, at the beach. It was just she and I, and we hadn't spent time like that since we were teenagers! I hadn't really kept my end of the relationship up or made any effort to visit her since I left home when I was 20. During this visit I realized we were each other's lifelines to our shared past and also, as it turns out, our dreams for the future.

Having both spent every summer together at the Shore for at least 15 of our first years, it turns out we both harbor the dream of living near the ocean. And just to prove it, we drove 7 hours out of Tennessee to the South Carolina shore to spend an entire week to ourselves. I think it was an attempt to recreate our summers at our Grandparent's shore house.

We spent hours talking about how we could ever make a move to the beach happen. And came up with so many reasons why it wouldn't work it was downright discouraging. Were we dreaming of returning to those childhood days? Probably.

"I'm still raising my kids, we just don't have the money, and I can't leave my job for at least another 10 years!" Karen sighed.

"Well, Tim and I've talked about it a lot. Now that I'm in a job I can take anywhere, and our kids are on their own, living at the beach is a bit more realistic. Maybe we could own it together and use it for vacations and rent it out the rest of time. But yeah, we don't have the money either, and we'd have to wait for Tim to retire." I sighed too.

It was a great idea, just not the right time. And even though Tim and I were slightly ahead of Karen and her husband, how could we possibly wait for another 10 years to get back to the ocean? We'd just rediscovered it!

We both took pictures of everything and each other. Karen even took a short 360-degree video of the beach, with the sand and the surf, shore homes, the umbrellas, people, and towels, and recorded the sound of the waves roiling up in a rhythmic, trance-inducing lullaby.

Karen told me in one of her post vacation text messages that she listens to it every morning.

Taking life one beautiful day at a time gives me instant gratification, as well as possibilities for the future. I have no doubt we'll live at the beach eventually. In the meantime, Karen and I listen to its recorded image, and dream of the surf at night. While I do my best to live in the present, I also realize that creating wonderful new memories to pull out and savor later is important too.

I daydream about the salt air that wafted through our windows during that glorious week and together Karen and I are planning our next summer vacation.

Adaptive Creativity

One of the most important lessons I've learned is that the world is constantly changing, and I must be willing to change along with it. Do I still fit into the universe? How? My worldview has changed to accommodate my ever-evolving place in society as I age and learn new things. I call the act of changing my thoughts, attitude or circumstances *adaptive creativity*, and it requires me to be mentally flexible.

An example might be taking a skill for writing and using it to write anything: technical, creative, fiction, non-fiction, persuasive, or descriptive. The same could be said for taking an education in Fine Art, and applying it to the study of Graphic Art. I define adaptive creativity as the ability to take what you already have and know and change or build on it to solve life's challenges. I might also describe it as taking an educated risk.

What happens when things don't turn out the way you'd like? You may have to adjust your timeline, or chose different opportunities. It doesn't mean you have to feel negatively about yourself or your circumstances.

It is a fact that we cannot control everything.

Journal Entry: Good News, Bad News

My Facebook comment today reads:

"Good News: Daily routine includes drawing, writing, treadmill and job hunting. Bad News: Job-hunting not successful to date. Good News: NY agent has agreed to review my manuscript.

Bad News: COBRA runs out at the end of this month.

Good News...."

There are ups and downs in everyone's life. Do we weigh each event and decide the cumulative result to be positive or negative, and then choose our attitude? I believe we are much more resilient than this. I like to think of successfully negotiating life's challenges as 'survival surfing.'

This is just another phrase for the creative adaptability that allows our right-brain to jump in and help us think of alternatives and options. Simply remembering we have options goes a long way towards quieting that first left-brain instinct to panic.

Defining Yourself

Throughout all of our family's financial challenges, time has marched unflinchingly forward. Tim and I lost our home just as the youngest of three and our last child at home moved out to pursue her own dreams. Not only was I no longer expected or required to nurture, protect or otherwise insert myself into my children's lives, everything in my world was in a state of flux.

I was cleaning out the house and relinquishing worldly goods, moving into a different part of the Valley around Phoenix, dealing with issues at work, and living for weeks with just our puppy in the new house while Tim traveled for his job. I also spent a year challenged by illness, hormonal changes and emotional breakdowns at work, which eventually cost me my job. It seemed to be an unending nightmare.

God and the Universe must have been watching over us. I unpacked into my new, smaller rental home, which I christened 'The Cottage' and set up my new studio corner. Daisy, our dachshund, and I spent evenings in our cozy home writing, drawing, reading and watching TV on the days Tim worked away from home.

With the final loss of my job, I discovered that life did not end. I was devastated, traumatized, and felt totally worthless, but the sun still continued to come up in the mornings.

Finally I became angry. I decided I had to move on or admit that I really was obsolete. I started a new project, one that I enjoyed and that made me feel good about myself: a blog to showcase my artwork and writing. As I continued to look for income, I renewed my commitment to using my creativity to find it.

> Don't sell yourself short! Don't allow anyone to make you feel obsolete, marginalized, or irrelevant.

I discovered that I could still define myself as a writer and artist, because I was still writing and making art. I did not, however, approach my life in the idealistic and unrealistic fashion I once did. I now knew more about my own survival skills.

I began to feel steady, balanced and confident. My blog, art, and writing all showcased the gifts I'd been blessed with. My general goal was to simply enjoy what I had. I decided to specialize in positive thinking and silver linings. My six-year-old inner artist began to celebrate.

Journal Entry: Glimmers of Recovery

It's now a week since I left work.

I've filed for unemployment and COBRA.

As I develop perspective, I begin to see it was the best thing to have happened.

Now that I have the time, I've been exploring and discovering places and resources around my home. I've found the local library and post office and coffee shop.

I spend time every day looking for a new job online. I'm looking not for just a new job, but a different direction. I'm now over 50, apparently too old to be 'smart' by younger standards and too young and too broke for retirement. Besides, what would I do in retirement? I'd be bored stiff!

When Enough is not Enough

Once you've defined your goals, examine them carefully. Are they inclusive of your family or partner? Will they provide you with self-fulfillment without sacrificing the blessings you already have but take for granted?

And what will you do when you accomplish those goals?

After surviving the end of a business and the loss of our home, my entire point of view changed. There is no disgrace in redefining your goals, or shifting your point of view based on learning something new about yourself.

Along the way I learned that attaining personal goals that didn't consider Tim or the children were worthless to me. My life wasn't just about money or personal recognition.

Journal Entry: Seeking Freedom

Sometimes I feel an overwhelming desire to slip the bonds of a reality that requires all of us to earn or otherwise have money to survive.

If money was out of the equation, I might:

1. Learn to play the violin. My brief career as a violist from age 8 to 18 was overshadowed by an almost-debilitating stage fright that made me physically ill before performing in public. The experience, however, left me with an aching love and deep appreciation for all string and bow music. This time I'd like to play the melody.

2. Abandon myself to great swathes of color on wall-sized canvas as an emotional outlet, without concession to public approval or funding.

3. Live in a cozy bungalow on a beach where I can open the bedroom windows at night and fall asleep and awaken to the rhythmic, soothing ebb and flow of water on the shore.

There is one intrinsic human need, however, that trumps all these desires, that above all else allows me to really flourish in this world despite its challenges.

It is something I am blessed to have found and honestly do not think I could live without: being the focus of another's love and coming first in someone else's life.

Because I've imagined the desires above, they may yet come to me. But I will not accept or pursue any of them at the cost of loosing my family. This is my own, personal rule, and an important consideration.

Keep in mind those who love you and if they are an important part of your life they will also need to be a part of your journey.

> Remember that money alone is not enough.

Living in Balance

Weighing self-centric goals against the compromise of a loving relationship with a life partner, or doing work that isn't completely your choice or passion in exchange for leisure time spent in pursuit of the desired activity, are choices we make everyday. Balancing your life between work or leisure, drudgery or joy, alone or in partnership, the worldly or spiritual, or whatever you find are the requirements for your own mental health, is another of my own lessons.

My dad used to tell us to partake of everything in moderation, or in other words, life isn't all work, or all play. I've discovered that for me, it means a balance between the two.

Remember to Have Fun!

Don't forget to enjoy life. Find your joy and complement your work with joyful events. Don't work to the exclusion of family and friends. We've been given an amazingly wonderful planet to live on, with beauty all around us in animals, plants and humans. Look for it, share it, and expect joy.

Laugh often. I was depressed as a teenager and I remember my grandmother telling me to smile more and I'd feel happier. I've discovered this to be true. If I can smile or laugh, I do find myself feeling better. And smiles and laughter are contagious. Like yawning, you might just be the source of a never-ending chuckle passed from one person to the next, and helping the world become a happier place.

> Expect joy and laugh often; it's contagious!

Play and Learn: Who Are You?

Once you've identified your life goal(s), and built up your self-confidence, how do you present yourself to the world? How you think about yourself is often how others think of you. I learned early on that if I couldn't seriously consider myself an artist then no one else would.

A recent approach to defining or re-defining what you do is to *brand* yourself. Treat yourself as if you were a business and establish a *look and feel* of what you can provide to society.

The following steps encouraged me to pull together an overall brand and each tool (resume, business card, email, blog, web posting) reflected that identity.

More than just a self-label, it is a reflection of everything you know about yourself. If you live as if your dream has been attained you'll begin to do all the things needed to reach it.

In my case my brand encompassed a creative personality with a unique combination of artistic and technical knowledge and skills, and translated into a byline of 'Artist and Writer.'

What is your byline? How do you define and apply your new sense of who you are to finding that perfect job or past time? Here are a few ideas to research.

1. Return to the exercise in Chapter One in which you developed your ME diagrams of what you would like to do.

2. Use a dry erase board, a corkboard, or Pinterest.com to create your own Design/Inspiration Board.

3. Use the words and ideas uncovered in your earlier ME diagrams, along with personal photos and magazine articles, or anything you find that inspires you to pursue your goals. Having them out and visible helps keep you motivated, focused and organized.

4. Pull together a list of skills you've acquired throughout your career or life experience that will apply to what you are interested in doing.

5. Some skills, like web and graphic design, can be demonstrated. An example of this would be having a passion for creating your own web sites, and using these as part of your portfolio.

6. Having visual samples of what you do well makes it much easier to present your skills to others.

7. Without spending money, set up a home office, studio, or closet and practice your 'craft.' Arrange your office or studio in a manner that pleases you. Try to arrange office or art supplies neatly, with your desk clean or work surface uncluttered.

   Be sure, if possible, to have a door to close so you can work away from the family, dirty dishes and the laundry. Often the mental benefits of simply clearing the kitchen table after the children go to bed and labeling it your writing space can be phenomenal.

8. Sell yourself. I'm not talking about trying to be something you aren't. I'm talking about discovering your self worth, owning your strengths and letting others know who you are. You are an important part of your product or service, and society. If you've suffered health or financial disaster, think about redefining yourself as a survivor, rather than a victim.

   The best way to sell anything is to believe in your product...you!

You are a valuable member of society and have unique contributions to make!

Chapter 6: Learning New Tricks

Organize Your Thoughts

Each of us has a stream of inner thoughts. How can you keep track of every brilliant idea or even the glimmers of new thoughts? Hopefully you've been taking notes about new discoveries, subjects, photos, and ideas in your Dream Journal. You should now have:

1. Your Dream Statement,

2. Your Dream Journal, a collection of notes and ideas,

3. ME diagrams of ideas about how to get there,

3. A description or idea of what environment you'd like to do it in,

4. A list of people in your supportive network,

5. Affirmation(s), mental images, and other tools to motivate you.

Organizing your thoughts and notes can be a challenge, but not impossible. If you've written everything into your Dream Journal you should be able to find specific notes again. The following tools can help you organize your most important ideas about how you are going to change your life:

-   Artist's or Mission Statement
-   Business or Project Plan

Artist Statement/Mission Statement

Once you've determined what direction you'd like to go in to solve your dilemma, write it out. Return to your Dream Statement in Chapter One.

How would you tweak this earlier statement to more accurately express your desired goals? If you are an artist, this will become your *Artist Statement.*

If you are starting your own business, make this your *Mission Statement.* Even if you are neither of these, a *Mission Statement for Your Life* will state your overall life's direction. Not only does this force you to define your goals, it lets others know what your goals and intentions are. Spell out how your intentions for the future will improve or advance your life.

This was my first *Mission Statement,* written in the late 1990's before the advent of my own business, Fallon Designs:

To be published and recognized in my field as an eloquent and expressive illustrator with a unique style, who has the ability to portray those precious moments in life which evoke feelings that people want to share and remember. To take this talent and become a highly respected and successful greeting card artist, from which I will earn enough money to help provide for my family without sacrificing valuable family time.

As I compare this previous statement to my Dream Statement introduced in Chapter One, you can see how limited in scope this earlier one was. The one following is what my Mission Statement has evolved into.

I, Wendy Fallon, am an artist and writer and am making art and writing to help others experience the beauty of life in and around them. I would like to have more joy, time for my family, financial security and less stress in my life.

Business/Project Plan: Nailing the Details

I cannot begin to tell you how many lists of tasks we wrote out and accomplished while planning the opening of the Gallery.

First, we had various other parties we had to work with. We needed a real estate agent to coordinate with the landlord of the space we had chosen. We had to find a bank for a business account and a line of credit, and an architect to draw up building plans of the space than then needed to be approved by the city of Chandler. A general contractor who would actually build out the space was required, and the artists with whom we needed to establish agreements for display space, studios, and art classes also had to be found.

Then there was collecting art for sale, the grand opening to plan, software to acquire and learn to manage our sales and bookkeeping. Establishing a budget based on as-yet-to-be-seen sales was a difficult task. Along with that came what seemed like a million decisions about the color of the wall paint, the color of ceiling paint, how to finish the floor, and choosing a set of kitchen appliances.

We couldn't have accomplished any of it without listing every step and determining the order in which to execute them. Setting goals and priorities, often based on money, time, and the needs of our families, was an important part of the process. All of these lists created records we could return to over and over throughout the birth of the Gallery.

Lists keep you organized and efficient. Using lists can help you accomplish anything! As a right-brain dominant personality, I've had to learn this skill.

A business or project plan is your roadmap for

accomplishing your goal. Organizing the lists you've made in your Dream Journal by topic is a start. By now you should have some idea of the steps involved in manifesting your dream.

Example: Acquire a business license, look for available space, rent or purchase office equipment, and other tasks. Placing these steps in a timeline is the next step. Sometimes it is easier to accomplish this on your computer.

If you are building a business plan, it is much better to have it documented electronically. You can then email it to whoever needs access to it. Go to the Internet and search for business plan templates.

These will give you an idea of what types of information to include. Most business plans include justification, descriptions and examples of businesses like the one you are proposing, which is important if you are planning to ask for a loan.

Your project plan consists of specific physical tasks that you and anyone you are consulting with will be responsible for. Formal business and project plans can be monumentally complex for extremely large projects (i.e. construction of large commercial buildings, etc) or informally simple. If your goal is additional education, a new career, or moving to a different part of the country, your plans will be customized to your goal and can be an informal list of tasks.

Organize Your Time

Setting Goals
How do you know if you're going in the right direction if

you don't have a map? What held true for the relatively short-term goal of opening the Gallery also holds true for taking a new direction in life. Your Dream Statement, which became your Mission Statement, also becomes your largest, overall goal.

Deciding on the largest, long-term goal, then breaking it down into smaller chunks of short and mid-term goals will help you stay focused, and organize your thoughts and time. Accomplishing the smaller, immediate tasks first will give you the confidence and encouragement to continue moving ahead.

Setting Priorities

One of the best practices I've ever learned is to set priorities. Once I've written out a list of tasks, I number them in order of priority. The higher the priority of a task, the sooner and more often I work at it for a longer period of time.

For instance, my number one goal in 2012 was to find income. To accomplish this goal, I spent time everyday Monday through Friday searching and applying for jobs online, reading the local newspaper, and researching writing opportunities. I determined a minimum number of applications to submit in a week and I created a daily working routine around this task. My *job* then was to find a job.

Continuing to work on my dream, however, was and still is, also important to me. I added additional time each day for writing, drawing and blogging. And this is the point. Finding time in your busy daily life for working towards your dreams or indulging in a hobby is important to your health and happiness and accomplishing the tasks needed to get there is imperative. My goal at that time was securing income from writing, drawing or blogging.

Play & Learn: Your Life Mission Statement & Plan

Now it's time to create your Mission Statement, Plan and Tasks.

1. Use your Dream Statement to define your overall final Goal. Your 'final' goal can be anything from a life-long pursuit, to simply finding a job you enjoy. I believe you have a higher chance of successfully attaining your short-term goals (i.e. a job) if they are in line with your long-term goals (i.e. a life-long pursuit, your biggest dream).

2. From your earlier ME diagrams write out a list of the major steps or activities you need to accomplish that will result in reaching your goals. You will have collected these steps from researching and learning about your desired goal.

3. Choose 3 major tasks as the most important for reaching your goal and number them 1 through 3.

4. Break each of these tasks into sub-tasks and list all the details you need to proceed under each one. If you are suffering from fear, list the easiest task first. Be sure to include regular discussions with your family for each task. I cannot guarantee that you will reach your final goal, but you will increase your chances of success by at least knowing what direction you want to move in. Treat this as a map with significant signposts. Celebrate and congratulate yourself when you complete each task, and share it with your family or your supportive network.

5. Once you've completed these first 3 tasks, chose the next 3 and repeat. If you feel stuck between tasks, return to your ME diagrams to see if you have missed any critical steps to reaching your goal. You may need to do more research about your chosen direction by visiting the library, searching online, or speaking to someone who is currently doing or has done in the past what you would like to do.

6. Always keep in mind that just because you reach your overall goal, doesn't mean that life stops. Be prepared to meet your goal and look towards the next. I'm already thinking about my next book.

Flexible Time Management

I have never been able to adhere to a rigid schedule.

My own time management skills have never been the best and are something I will always need to work on. But I do like accomplishing goals, and have discovered that setting too many at once makes me feel overwhelmed and discouraged even before I start. So my approach has morphed into what I call 'flexible' time management. It has nothing to do with procrastination or being lazy. It has everything to do with the level of stress I've determined to accept into my life.

I make lists. I establish my larger goal first and then break it into three to four chunks of short to mid-term goals. I list everything I need to accomplish under each of these manageable smaller goals, choose one to start on and work toward completing it every day. If I don't complete the entire list of these smallest tasks in a single day or week I don't worry about it.

Sometimes I decide to complete 3 tasks each day. It helps to set an allotted amount of time each day. My short term goals, believe it or not, include mundane tasks like doing the dishes every day, giving my allergic dog her twice-a-week medicated baths, or planning for upcoming family birthdays. I sometimes feel that if I can't keep myself organized enough to take care of everyday life tasks, I'll never feel organized or confident enough to accomplish my dreams.

I try not to sweat the small stuff, like a sink full of dirty dishes. As my mother used to say, the housework will always be there. I'm much more attracted to the creative tasks on my list, but getting started is my biggest stumbling block.

Starting tasks for short-term goals, like researching drawing techniques, creating a pair of seashell earrings for a gift, or designing a page layout, can still be intimidating. In my case, I give myself a couple of chunks of time to prepare for starting the task. For instance, in a 15-minute period I can clear off my work surface and arrange my work tools within easy reach. I can choose the materials I want to use or search the Internet and print directions for the art method I'd like to use.

Breaking the starting tasks down into 15-minute chunks allows me to walk into my studio for a longer period of time, sit down, and begin immediately.

At the other extreme, there are some things that may become on-going pursuits. These are mid- to long-term goals. An example of a long-term goal is my intention to continue writing. I don't plan to write a certain number of pages each day but instead may turn out anywhere from 300 to 2,000 words in each sitting. The most important criteria is that I don't stop. I still use lists for these longer goals, of course, and each writing project evolves from an extensive outline.

What I have learned is that not everyone works at the same pace and with the same priorities.

There are those who are very high energy, live on caffeine and simply don't know how to slow down. These high-energy types can also be extremely detail-oriented. They work their projects from the inside out by creating detailed chunks of finished tasks. The details are worked out first and then assembled into a comprehensive whole. Others, like me, set a slower, steadier pace and work from the outside in. I envision the completed concept or the big picture first and identify the detailed parts second.

Play & Learn: Finding Motivation

Getting started and staying on task, especially for the mid- and long-term goals can be difficult. Your high level of commitment will help, but sometimes it's easy to lose sight of what you are trying to accomplish. There are a million ways to get sidetracked and lose momentum.

- If your lists are too long, you might start to feel discouraged. This might be because you've broken your tasks into too many tiny tasks that don't seem to be getting you anywhere. Try grouping several together by day so you feel a sense of accomplishment.

- If you don't schedule enough tasks during a week, or feel a lack of accomplishment, you may drop your goals altogether. The trick is to turn your task time into a habit, so you accomplish a steady amount of work on a regular basis.

- Perhaps you're not sure where to start. List your tasks in order of priority.

- To get yourself started, do your prep in 15-minute chunks. Give yourself a deadline. Make an appointment with yourself to actually sit down and just get started. Then set a timer for 15-minutes, even though you've allotted two to three times that amount. Commit to the first 15 minutes, and if for whatever reason you can't continue, allow yourself to stop until the next time.

  Very often that 15 minute start will get you so involved that you'll turn off the timer and keep right on going for the entire time allotted.

  By the way, this also works with getting the dishes and housework done.

- Share your goals with others who support you. If you've committed to a task that you've shared with others, you'll be more likely to complete it.

- Think about what it will be like once you've accomplished a long-term goal. Sharing your sense of accomplishment and excitement with your supporters will give a feeling of immense satisfaction and self-confidence.

Organize Your Space
A Place to Live, Dream, Work

I spent several years studying architecture. One of the most fascinating concepts I discovered was not just designing the exterior of a building and it's interior space, but the *environment* of the exterior and interior spaces and the neighborhood around it. My philosophy concerning architectural design is that it should be a holistic approach that will create the optimum enjoyment and functional use of that building.

Along with this, I learned that there are many variables that affect the enjoyment of a completed building; orientation to the sun, light and dark spaces; textures, sound, color, landscaping, height of the ceilings, entrance and egress, traffic patterns, parking layout, and the list goes on. The study of how all of these variables affect humans is sometimes called environmental psychology.[8]

Although you may not feel the need to know this much about why we spend more time in one space rather than another, organizing your spaces according to function can help you accomplish your goals.

For instance, I found it to my benefit to separate my living space from my dreaming space. Dedicating a corner in which to sit comfortably, out of the mainstream of the home, with good natural light in which to draw and write, encouraged me to spend time in that space.

---

[8] Tony Hiss, *The Experience of Place* (New York, NY: Vintage books, a division of Random House, Inc., 1990).

It was also a commitment on my part that I would spend time pursuing my dreams.

My studio is made up of the colors, textures, materials and objects that encourage me to create. It contains all of my favorite things.

Another division of space to consider might be setting aside the place in which you pay the bills, call the doctor, make appointments, and balance the checkbook. I now know I cannot do these things in my studio and still expect to be creative in that same space.

So even if you live in a one-room studio, choosing the best corner with the best light in which to read, write, draw, paint, craft or otherwise pursue your dreams will be encouraging.

Play & Learn: Organizing Your Space

In what space will you pursue your dreams? No matter how small your living space, you can still designate a space for dreaming, writing, practicing your craft, painting, etc. If your goal is to move into a new space in which to pursue your dreams, what will that space look like? Here are a few suggestions.

1.   Return to your Dream Journal and find the information you added to your ME diagrams, and perhaps the photos you've collected on Pinterest.com, concerning the colors, textures, fabric, and furniture you envisioned in your creative space.

2.   Draw a rectangle the size of your page to serve as your imaginary floor plan, or draw out the floor plan of space you have available to you.

Using block shapes, arrange your chosen furniture in your creative space and use markers or any medium of your choice to add colors representing the walls, floors or rugs.

3. If you have a computer, there are websites and software that will allow you to do this online. Creating it in your Dream Journal, however, will give you the hands-on overall feeling as well as keep all your goal-oriented information in one place.

4. Think about storage, supplies, and equipment.

5. Pick up a magazine at the bookstore or library about home studios. The studios profiled are amazing and reflect the creativity of the person working and playing in them.

6. For more ideas, browse the Internet or Pinterest.com for small space organizational ideas, interior design, and work and play environments.

7. Re-purpose found or used furniture to fit your needs.

Organize Your Life's Work

Here are two examples of how to present your achievements, education and experience. A portfolio can be used to organize visual projects as well as projects completed for clients. A resume will list your employment, education and skill set. Some individuals have created both and are prepared to present them at each interview.

These two approaches are also excellent ways to record, archive or otherwise document dates and projects you may not always remember.

One of the easiest ways of deciding what to present to a prospective employer is to know and be able to access all of your life's experience and then choose the achievements and skills that are relevant to the job you are applying for. There are several books on the market and tutorials on the Internet that will show you how to format both types of information for presentation.

Portfolio

Artist's (graphic artists, architects, etc) portfolios have traditionally been composed of printed samples or slides of artwork along with an artist's statement and a list of exhibits you may have participated in. As technology moves at lightning speed into the future of digital media, many artists have discovered the convenience of posting their portfolios to a website. There are community web sites that will do this for you for a subscription fee.

If you don't consider yourself an artist, having an online presence for whatever your passion or means of self-expression is can still be beneficial.

It definitely helps to have samples of your work, whatever it is, somewhere online where a potential employer or client can find it. Your web address, or URL, should go in your email signature and on your business cards. And yes, you should have both, even if you don't have your own business.

If you are like me and don't want to pay or don't have the money for online hosting services, try starting a blog.

There are several that are still free (www.Wordpress.com and www.Blogspot.com are the best known.) Not only can you then reference your blog address, you can easily add artwork to it yourself without the services of a web master.

One drawback to this alternative is the risk of someone claiming your work as their own or using it without your permission. Always be sure to include the copyright sign (©), and your name beside anything you post to the Internet or a copyright notice on each page. Another alternative is to watermark your work. An additional option is to register your work with the U.S. Copyright Office (www.copyright.gov). This may not deter thieves, but it will give you the legal grounds to sue them.

I've always believed that the simpler the web design, the better it showcases visual art. Online web site pages can be works of art themselves, or can be chosen from several well-designed templates. The goal is to obtain the widest exposure possible for your work, or samples of your self-expression, and to provide a place where prospective employers, patrons and gallery owners, or clients can go to view your work. In the most general sense, it is one way to share your gift with as many people as possible.

Resume

Depending on how you plan to use your resume, placing it online will provide you with a location to send prospective employers or clients to in addition to posting it to job sites like Jobing.com, Dice.com, SimplyHired.com, or Indeed.com.

If you are an artist, adding a resume to your portfolio adds additional background for employers.

Writers, dancers, musicians, or anyone else can benefit from having an online visual or photographic presence. Yes, you are throwing your information out into the digital world. No, you may not be able to get it back.

It goes without saying that anything you present to promote yourself should be free of spelling or grammatical errors and easy to read.

Play & Learn: Seeking Income

Seeking employment during or after a debilitating recession is tough. Seeking employment during a recession if you've been laid off from a life-long career is even tougher. I cannot guarantee that anything I've written here will win you a new job, but here are a few ideas.

1. If you are unable to find work in your industry, consider a different but related industry.

2. Consider moving from office work to a vocational job. If it requires returning to school, think of ways to obtain new training.

3. If you like working with computers, consider obtaining certifications from Microsoft or the manufacturer of your favorite major software.

4. If you cannot find work in your area, and your family isn't adverse to moving or having you commute, look for work elsewhere.

5. Create your own job. If you have an idea or hobby, use it as the basis for a business.

Use your right-brain thinking and brainstorm outside of the ordinary. This is easy for me to write, but I am aware of how difficult it can be to find work.

Staying busy and connected to your community can be a challenge and finding involvement outside of the comfort zone of your previous job might be the last thing you feel like doing. Persevere!

If you are passed midlife and looking for income, what kind of skills can you provide a younger generation? What would you like to learn more of; carpentry, flying, teaching someone to read? Consider teaching a class in your community at the local library in your area of expertise.

I've read about grandmothers who've had their grandchildren videotape them while cooking, and posting the videos to YouTube.com along with recipes. Have your children or grandchildren show you how to use the latest technology.

If you can demonstrate anything, there are others out there who want to learn.

Building Your Platform

Another tool for selling yourself, your skills or your product is a platform. Your platform is your online presence. It reflects your brand, your services, examples of your work, your resume, and any advertising or marketing you do.

It can include your blog, Facebook.com fan page, and your postings to Twitter. It may present your opinions or experiences related to your art or passion. The best platforms will show a consistent look and feel and will also reflect your brand.

You can build your platform slowly, adding social media and building a client or patron list as you develop a business.

Creative Employment

Once you have the tools mentioned previously in place, it is time to exercise your creativity. You most likely are not looking for a traditional, corporate job. You are looking for something unusual, exciting, and that your combination of creative skills, knowledge and experience make you uniquely qualified for.

In earlier chapters you have hopefully identified a new direction in which to move and uncovered a forgotten dream, past-time or hobby. Was it something you were particularly good at, or happy doing in the past?

Play & Learn: Who is Your Audience or Market?

When seeking creative employment, consider how you can apply your passion and goals to resolve a need. Determining who your market is and how you can provide an answer to what they are looking for may yield opportunities.

1. Use your skill to promote concern for the environment. A talented landscape photographer I know has started promoting the importance of keeping our environment healthy for the wildlife that inhabits it.

2. Teach a how-to class within your community about your passion. It could be about anything, i.e. refurbishing cars, mosaics, researching on the Internet, knitting, etc.

3. Look for work that helps a cause, i.e. volunteer at the local animal shelter or Veterans Administration.

Volunteering has become the overlooked opportunity. Demonstrating your reliability, willingness to learn and work, and past experience sometimes leads to a job offer. At the very least, you will learn what training you need to seek a permanent position.

4.   If you are skilled at a craft, consider posting your work for sale on Etsy.com, a web site on which shoppers find all kinds of handmade items.

One young lady I know supports herself and her young son by maintaining a vibrant business online designing and providing unique, handcrafted baby wear, which allows her to be at home to raise her child.

Take a holistic approach to your life. Re-visit your Dream Statement from Chapter One. Is it still consistent with the direction you've decided on? Does your portfolio and resume, your list of things to do to attain the change in your life you are seeking, the environment you live in and the work you want to do reflect your Dream Statement?

Don't give up!

Chapter 7: The Importance of Art

The Importance of Art and Community

By investigating your own creativity and how it affects your community you can learn how important your creative contributions are to society.

Why is it so important that we as a society strive to add more right-brain creativity into our lives? Let's look at the current challenges facing the world today: global financial distress, increased political polarity, the discovery of antibiotic-proof illnesses, and loss of home-ownership, just to name a few. In my opinion, humans have always had challenges to our survival. And we've always found answers.

They may not have been the answers we as individuals were looking for, but many of our societal threats have been resolved. In my case, my husband and I lost the ownership of our home, and found a rental. We still have a roof and a home to live in. When the Gallery shut down I was able to obtain employment. And as the global economy continued to slide, countries around the world attempted to work together to keep a minimum financial infrastructure intact. None of these answers, on a personal or global level, are easily swallowed or manifested. Many solutions come with a cost and most with compromise.

We do, however, as a species, have a secret weapon. Each of us has a survival mechanism that allows us to think our way out of most catastrophes. Art, in its own way, encourages the use and development of this ability to find our way towards survival and a happier existence. Thinking creatively encourages us, not to come up with one answer, but with many possible solutions.

If we as individuals can access more of our right-brain functions and improve our own existence, as well as that of our community, won't we eventually solve the larger ones as well?

Children and Art

Why is teaching your children how to make art important? I am reminded of the art classes I was lucky enough to have during my education.

With some projects we were encouraged to create at least three designs that all fulfilled the requirements of the exercise. I hated it because I felt that the first idea I came up with was always my best. It wasn't until I studied architecture that I realized that we all have the ability to create more than one solution to every problem, and how important this was.

Making art exercises creative abilities, and teaches children from a young age not only that self-expression is their right, but that they have the ability to come up with their own answers and solutions.

Our children are the engineers, doctors, and professionals of tomorrow that we rely on to solve the world's dilemmas through creative thought. Imagine how limited a world we'd live in if the first idea was the only right answer?

> The first idea is rarely the only right answer.

Adults and Art

As adults, we can take a lesson from our children and delight in the freedom of self-expression. Studies have been made of the affects of making art on the overall health of an aging population. It has been determined that making art is a positive activity for the elderly. It seems that when we begin to lose our mental capacity for memory, we expand in creativity.

I am not a medical expert, but wouldn't it be amazing if making art exercised the right-brain to the point of improving an aging mental attitude and allowing us to live happier and healthier lives?

In fact, because of increasing longevity, there will soon be the need to determine what to do with ourselves once society has decided we've passed our mental peak. Unfortunately these determinations are based on the obsolete social convention of retirement. We are now at the beginning of a new social strata comprised of those of us who are too young to collect social security and too old to be hired into the mainstream corporate environment. Living longer and the recent recession have created the need for creative income.

Older workers no longer employed or who are convinced of their obsolescence carry with them a mature, broader point of view and two-thirds of a lifetime of experience. This time in our lives may hold opportunities for providing solutions to society that will also give us income and purpose. Finding that income and purpose is a creative exercise that requires commitment, motivation, inspiration, and creative thought.

As a direct result of the recent recession and the aging of the Baby Boomer generation, there are fewer jobs, less pay, and more of us competing for employment. The younger generations aren't being hired into jobs because older generations are holding onto them longer. On an individual level, creativity is and will be an increasing requirement for finding employment and income.

Business and Art

The effect of art on business, especially on abandoned urban areas of the United States can be seen in the migration of financially healthy businesses.

Before the Great Recession, performance and visual art was seen as an attraction for young, upwardly mobile, well-educated professionals wanting to live and work in an area where there were cultural activities[9]. Within these populations small businesses flourished, and larger businesses expanded.

Seattle, Washington demonstrated this during the last century by offering a culturally rich environment in the form of art, theater, the Fish Market, and small shops. These small businesses were in turn supported by the highly educated employees brought into the area by large technology corporations. Microsoft® was one of these.

More recently, when our latest recession struck in 2008, workers, irrespective of their education or standard of living, lost their jobs and homes. Many workers lost their feelings of security, the ability to survive and flourish, and confidence in national and global infrastructures. Young degree holders without experience found it increasingly difficult to find that all-important first job, and experienced older professionals close to retirement were downsized and sacrificed to the corporate bottom line. Small businesses disappeared overnight.

---

9 Richard Florida, *The Rise of the Creative Class* (New York, NY: Basic Books, a member of the Perseus Books Group, 2002).

The luxury of choosing an area to live and work in became almost nonexistent. Workers were faced with going to where the work was, if any, regardless of the presence of a cultural environment. Art in the public school systems became, and still is, less of a priority and more of a financial burden. In many school districts it is still one of the first subjects to be eliminated.

Although housing values may not return to their previously over-inflated value, and jobs may not pay the same as expected before the recession, we, individually and as a society, will survive. Art and creative thought will never disappear, and the more each of us exercise our right-brain thinking to solve our society's lack of income, food, and shelter, the sooner we'll return to fiscal health and happier lives. It's happening already.

As the economy begins to turn around, artists may again take up residence in the depressed urban areas in which they can afford to live and work in large, abandoned interior spaces. Artists have traditionally been the first to reclaim and re-purpose buildings that may have become part of urban decay. As these buildings are redesigned to fit the needs of the creative individuals who claim them, property values may increase and the cycle of urban rebirth will hopefully begin again.

One example of a re-purposed space that I visited in the heart of the city of Phoenix was once an auto-repair yard. A talented and successful metal sculptor turned it into the working studio of his dreams, with enough space to create yard-sized, three-dimensional shapes. (www.kevincaron.com)

Play & Learn: Art in Your Community

Everyday I see examples of creative thinking and ingenuity. Here are a few examples to think about.

1. Share art with children. See if your school system offers a program in which parents and other adults can volunteer to present and teach about the artwork of the old masters or try out one of Google's offerings, GoogleArtProject.com.

2. Learn about your community. One of the most popular forms of exercise among all ages today is walking. If your area of expertise is walking or hiking, consider taking or creating a walking tour in your town or city. Does your area offer historic locations, abundant wildlife, gardens, or bird watching? Take a walk around your neighborhood and look for new learning experiences.

3. Read the newspaper to find everyday examples of creative solutions. An article that caught my eye profiled a new type of business with a unique use of abandoned space. In the deteriorating stockyards of Chicago, a small company has taken over a warehouse and turned it into a hydroponics farm.

   They raise fish and plants for the restaurant industry. The premise is that used water containing fish waste is used to water and fertilize the plants. Along with a series of pipes, the plants cleanse the water, which is then returned to the fish tanks (www.312ap.com/home.)

   Re-purposing buildings and creating processes and new businesses like this require creative thinking.

> Don't discount your own ideas no matter how strange you think they may be. They might be the answer to someone else's question.

Sharing & Giving Back

Sometimes I imagine sitting out in space, watching humanity run around on a blue and green sphere and I wonder if we've ever mastered the gift of sharing. It always seems to me that sharing prosperity in times of economic hardship would be a global benefit.

Without delving into the mind-bending confusion of politics, let's examine the human motivation behind charity. How is giving back, aside from good karma, related to living a more creative, fulfilling life?

On one hand, some of us believe that sharing anything (money, time, clothing, books, skills, etc) is the same as giving away the farm. You've worked hard to get where you are, and what you have may not even be adequate for your own family.

Why give any of it away?

On the other hand, there are so many ways of thinking and living generously, all of which come out of positive thought and energy. Volunteering time to work with children teaches them generosity. Collecting and donating gently used clothing and household items not only provides much-needed items, but also creates jobs. And positive thought and energy are contagious. By giving back, you encourage others to give back. You may also be the motivating inspiration for those who need someone to believe in their personal worth and potential. Sometimes the gift of your time is the best encouragement someone can receive.

In the end, sharing your good fortune or positive energy only increases the overall good fortune of the world you live in. Everyone benefits.

> Giving back to and learning about your local community is the first step in the acceptance of cultural diversity.

What would happen if each of us made it a goal to simply do something nice for someone else each day? As overwhelming as some social issues are, bringing attention to them might be the first step towards resolution.

> Don't ever underestimate the value of your efforts simply because you are only one person.

While at the Gallery, Laurie and I participated in one of the first *Go Red for Women* campaigns. We asked for submissions of small, heart-related work from local artists, sold it in a special event within the Gallery, and donated a percentage of the sales to benefit women's heart health. Proceeds from the sales of other Gallery exhibits also went regularly to *Free Arts of Arizona*, which gives low-income and homeless children access to art activities and education.

Everyday I hear of individuals who are helping others. What a wonderful use of positive energy!

Play & Learn: Giving Back

Look around your community for opportunities to volunteer, for example:

1. Teach a free class at your local community center.

2. Serve hot meals at a project for the homeless.

3. Pick up litter in your favorite city park.
4. Offer to take an elderly neighbor to a doctor's appointment.

You will be amazed at what you will learn about your community and your neighbors, and in what ways you may find to use your creative skills to make your neighborhood, and the world, a better place.

To Retire...or not?

Even if you've lost or left your job, what do you want to do with the rest of your life? I personally cannot stand the idea of sitting around doing nothing and will most likely be employed at least part-time, earning an income or volunteering for a long time past 'retirement' age. However, it will be on my own terms, i.e. according to my Dream Statement. My activities both for income and leisure will be portable to allow for travel and I'll be able to do them from anywhere.

> Why not enjoy a productive life for every precious minute we've been allotted?

Chapter 8: Case Studies for Meaningful Work

Defining 'Work'

What is your definition of meaningful work? I know that mine is anything that falls within my Dream Statement. Definitions will be as unique to each of us as there are humans in the world. How you get there is your own personal journey. Here are a few steps in my own journey.

Fallon Designs

Established as a sole proprietorship in 2005, Fallon Designs was me. I offered fine and graphic art, and writing for print and the Web. My clients ranged from an aerial photography company for which I wrote trade magazine articles, to a private client who commissioned me to paint an original watercolor for his parents' wedding anniversary.

A sole proprietorship is a business with one owner and no other employees. I was the accountant, the bookkeeper, and the marketing director and, in addition to all this, I produced the service and product with my own hands. I enjoyed working with my clients to determine their needs and defining cost. My time and company decisions were my own.

What became increasingly difficult was finding new work and completing existing work at the same time. I spent an equal amount of time on both. I also did not make enough income to replace the corporate income or medical insurance I'd walked away from.

However, Fallon Designs taught me several valuable lessons. I developed my self-confidence and belief in my own creative skills. People liked what I delivered and I began to collect a fan base and a network of patrons for my artwork, which I still have. And I began to have glimmers of what could go into a book like this.

Art on Boston Gallery

Art on Boston was organized as a limited liability corporation (LLC) partnership. My business partner and I learned a lot of negative things about commercial rental contracts, as well as (over) supply and (poor) demand in the art industry and during the beginning of a recession. There were, however, a balance of, if not more, positive lessons as well.

An LLC does not always limit your liability, or protect you from all legal challenges. When the Gallery closed, we were appalled to find that the landlord could and might sue us for the remaining one year of rent. When we started out, of course, we did not intend to cut our lease short. We had hoped that because the business was closing due to the recession, we wouldn't be personally or individually responsible for some of our debt. Of course we were. Fortunately, the owner was more than generous and forgave the broken contract.

There were many more pros than cons. The community of local artists we pulled together was a miracle of creative inspiration and motivation. The space itself served all of downtown Chandler and we often opened the sliding glass panels at the front of the Gallery to encourage the public to visit. Visitors enjoyed artist demonstrations and free children's art activities.

The Gallery itself was composed of exhibit space, studios and classrooms. The artists who exhibited and worked in the space were encouraged to teach their medium as well.

We offered a different exhibit each quarter, along with an Exhibit Opening on the first night that was open and free to the public. It was like throwing a party in the brightest, most elegantly embellished space ever seen. We always had live music and refreshments.

I learned to design, document and teach my own classes, *Beginning Drawing: For Adults Who Think They Can't* being one of several.

Partnership was another lesson learned. Even though we each worked at different speeds, and disagreed on many things about how to run the Gallery, we did have complementary skills and enjoyed the synergy of making art together. For example, my business partner was by trade a journalist and handled the marketing and news releases. I designed and maintained the web site. These were only two of a myriad of tasks required to keep the Gallery running.

I will never regret opening the Gallery. I believe that the act of designing and building it, and taking the risk to attempt it, set an example for my own children. Each of them has followed their dreams with a fair amount of creativity of their own. That willingness to open and run a business has also contributed to my resume.

This is what my father said about regret:

'If, if and be-gosh darn!
If a hop-toad had wings,
He wouldn't bump his fanny on the sidewalk.'
(author unknown)

We cannot change history or predict the future. What we can

do is live a balanced life in the present to the best of our ability.

Embrace, own, cherish and celebrate your life!

Living Defiantly Creative in an Increasingly Unpredictable World

So, after a journey of several years, I've learned enough about what I and my inner artist need and have arranged my life accordingly. As a result, the criteria for my most recent employment included several parameters. As in any design challenge, it was, and still is, my job to design a solution, or possibly several, that meet all of my requirements.

1. My marriage and family would stay intact. This included not relocating, no strange hours and nothing that risked our financial security.

2. I would earn enough money to help pay the bills and still contribute to retirement.

3. It had to be a job I felt ethically at peace with.

4. It had to be a job that didn't cause a high level of stress. For example, commuting in over-crowded rush hours, or working in a politically or emotionally charged atmosphere. I now work from home and love it.

5. I knew I preferred project-oriented over hourly-oriented tasks.

6. Finally, it had to be a job that I was good at and enjoyed. It had to allow me enough energy after work hours and on the weekends to make my own art, i.e. painting, drawing, writing, or whatever activity I enjoyed.

Journal Entry: Re-employment

I can't believe it! I just received an email from a past co-worker, who had heard from another past co-worker, who is looking for a technical writer! The hiring manager is someone I worked for at least eight years ago, and who now works as an executive manager for a global company. If he hires me, it will be, once again, a miracle...I couldn't make this stuff up!

It took four months to arrange, with calls to and from the hiring manager, phone interviews with the team members I would be working with, and prayers every night that the position would be approved. The job would be technical writing with a global team, from my home office and at a generous pay with benefits.

At first I was afraid I wouldn't be able to meet their requirements. Once gain, my nemesis, FEAR, raised it's ugly head. Overcoming that fear, and pursuing this employment was a conscious decision I had to make.

The Universe, all of my work experience up to that point, good and bad, and all of the positive energy I had invested during my un-employment, was in my favor, and I was hired! I was once more employed with a regular paycheck and benefits, but without the stress of a cubicle or micromanagement, rush hour traffic, or office politics. And I've enjoyed it from the first day.

Remember my Dream Statement?

I, Wendy Fallon, am an artist and writer and am making art and writing to help others experience the beauty of life in and around them. I would like to have more joy, time for my family, financial security and less stress in my life.

Although my life hasn't worked out exactly the way I imagined, it has exceeded my expectations. Amazingly, I am so happy with my nine to five job that I have enough energy after work and on the weekends to indulge in my passion for making art and I now have a drawing student whom I teach on the weekends. That my dream statement matches reality so closely is, yes, a miracle!

Have I settled? I don't think so. I still spend time refining my dream of writing my own words, making my own art and making a livable wage and a generous retirement. It is important to me to continue to have a dream.

Is my life and marriage now perfect? Of course not. Do we still get sick, argue, struggle over money or priorities? Of course we do. If we didn't, it would be a dull existence indeed. But we are armed with the awareness that each of us has enough creativity to work through our challenges, individually and together.

Have I found my dream job? In most aspects, yes. I am continually learning more about what my goal looks like.

However, currently I have more joy, less stress, time for my family, and financial security. All this has translated into a beautiful balance between family, work and play. I wouldn't have attained any of these without the aid of my problem-solving skills and the creative thought that is my inner artist.

And if I can do it, so can you.

Play & Learn: ME Diagrams #2

Return to the first Play and Learn – ME Diagrams in Chapter One. On a clean page in your Dream Journal recreate your ME Diagram.

- Have your colors changed?

- Have your activities changed?

- Are you now able to add definitive dreams of what you would like to do, change or pursue?

- Have you answered any questions you might have had at the beginning of this book?

- Have you learned anything new about yourself?

- Have you been able to think of ways to overcome any challenges in your life by listening to your inner artist?

Even if all you have are more questions, remember that the first step to finding the answers is asking the questions in the first place. If you feel this book has helped you in any way, I'd love to hear from you at 6yearartist@gmail.com.

Chapter 9: Celebrating the Creative Life

I would like to share with you the experiences of individuals I feel live happier, richer lives through creative strength and thought. Each has found a way to incorporate some sort of self-expression into their everyday lives, part time or full time, as a professional or amateur. By sharing their stories, my goal is to provide you with the hope and motivation you need to change or improve your life.

Diana Alsip, Artist & Photographer

WF: What do you do?

DA: I am a 2D artist that works in the mediums of photography, paint, colored pencil, and pastel. Sometimes combined, but usually used individually. Most of my art explores the concept of "home;" where is it, what is it, is this a constructed notion, or one we carry inherently?

WF: Do you earn an income doing this? If not, would you do this if you didn't have to work?

DA: No; But if given the chance I would like to earn a living with my work.

WF: Has your creative skill improved your life? If so, how?

DA: Yes; I believe a creative mind is better able to adapt to changing situations. We are able to problem solve swiftly, which can lend itself to almost any career. We are survivors.

WF: My premise is that 'making art' uses right-brain resources, which strengthens creativity and creative thought, which in turn improves issue resolution and problem solving. Give one example in which you've had to overcome a personal or family challenge that has forced you to think outside of the box, or outside your comfort zone, to come up with a custom tailored resolution.

DA: My example is a selfish one, and solely caters to my own desires. I wanted to travel abroad, and instead of working hard and eventually saving enough to do so, I took a job teaching English as a second language in South Korea. It gave me the freedom to travel elsewhere, as well as experience life in another country.

Marian Crane, Mixed Media Artist & Writer

WF: What do you do?

MC: I make beaded and silver jewelry, leather masks, book art sculptures in various media, fiber art tapestries, and wearable art including theatrical and media costumes. I paint on canvas or paper with acrylics, as well as with digital art media including Corel Painter 12. I also write non-fiction and fiction, and have recently sold short stories and novels.

WF: Do you earn an income doing this? If not, would you do this if you didn't have to work?

MC: All of my living comes from creative endeavors, with 70% from commercial art applications and 30% from fine arts and crafts.

WF: Has your creative skill improved your life? If so, how?

MC: I could not function without exercising my creativity every day. Other than the therapy benefits, I'm happy to say that constantly honing my skills and learning new ones gives me a sense of self-worth, and some needed insulation from negative people and incidents.

WF: My premise is that 'making art' uses right-brain resources, which strengthens creativity and creative thought, which in turn improves issue resolution and problem solving. Give one example in which you've had to overcome a personal or family challenge that has forced you to think outside of the box, or outside your comfort zone, to come up with a custom tailored resolution.

MC: After trying to interest 68 literary agents in a big science-fiction manuscript, I put that project aside and wrote a romance novel just for fun.

I'd been uncertain about the genre, but learned that I loved it, and did well at it. Well enough that I leveraged a publisher's contract offer into an introduction to a very high-powered literary agent usually unavailable to unsolicited queries. Using the romance novel as almost a loss-leader, I now have representation for my other writing. If I hadn't been creative and bold, I'd still be stuck with the first manuscript.

Bonnie Lou Coleman, Artist & Musician

WF: What do you do?

BLC: I have a Masters in Music, ASU. I'm the former Director of Guitar Programs - Glendale Community College and ASU West. I currently maintain a few private classical guitar students and occasionally perform. I am the founder and former Director of the Phoenix Conservatory of Music and the Community School of the Arts, CSA- Art on Boston (now closed).

I maintain a studio of private art students; many of whom started studying with me at CSA almost five years ago. I primarily paint in acrylic and explore new passions regularly, i.e. paintings of classic cars, astronomical events, animals, sunflowers and seascapes. I also create mask, puppets, sock monkeys and creatures, sew creative hats, crochet, design beaded jewelry, explore polymer clay, and challenge myself to make useful and artistic items from recycled material.

WF: Do you earn an income doing this? If not, would you do this if you didn't have to work?

BLC: I have a small income from private lessons and occasional contracts for art classes in the schools, local hospitals, galleries and community centers. I also charge a fee for occasional public classical guitar performances.

I would create art and music whether I was paid for it or not- and do, constantly. I have a driving passion to create and be a dedicated teacher. I can only "work" a few hours a week due to my physical disability but creating art keeps my mind sharp, and busy, even when my body is uncooperative.

WF: Has your creative skill improved your life? If so, how?

BLC: Yes! I started painting again as a way to keep my mind off the pain and depression of losing my hard-won guitar career and high lifestyle after becoming permanently disabled. My creative pursuits give me purpose.

WF: My premise is that 'making art' uses right-brain resources, which strengthens creativity and creative thought, which in turn improves issue resolution and problem solving. Give one example in which you've had to overcome a personal or family challenge that has forced you to think outside of the box, or outside your comfort zone, to come up with a custom tailored resolution.

BLC: After a horrific bicycle accident in 1999, (when among other things, both thumbs were broken) I was forced to retire from teaching classical guitar at the colleges. I quickly realized how much of my life, and personality, were entwined with my professional career.

I also suffered a hard blow when my, newly diagnosed, bio polar husband decided that he didn't want me anymore since I was now permanently disabled and no longer top in my field! I suffered a deep depression while I went through a frightening divorce, severe income loss, eleven painful corrective surgeries, limited physical recovery and personal loss.

Fortunately I studied art as a child and throughout my college career, always choosing art classes as electives. I needed to supplement my income, (social security is below the poverty line), so I began taking on private students in my home studio and an awesome local gallery. This was a perfect solution for someone with limited mobility and an unfortunate requirement to maintain a low, protective, profile. When I connected with the local artistic community, it saved my life!

Bonnie Lou can be reached at
http://www.facebook.com/BonnieLouArt.

Laurie Fagen, Visual & Performing Artist, Writer

WF: What do you do?

LF: I "paint with fabric, words and musical notes" - I am a fiber and quilt artist, jewelry artist, art promoter, jazz singer and writer.

I design and create wearable art such as one-of-a-kind vests; I design and create contemporary art quilts; I design and create jewelry made from polymer clay, metal clay and commercial beads; I promote fine art and fine artists with a website and by offering Arizona-made artwork at various art galleries and retail shops in the Phoenix metro area; I perform classic jazz tunes with a keyboard player in various restaurants and jazz festivals; and as a long-time writer of non-fiction, I am writing mystery stories and making my short story mystery fiction debut in an Arizona anthology produced by Desert Sleuths, the Phoenix chapter of the international Sisters in Crime for female mystery writers.

WF: Do you earn an income doing this? If not, would you do this if you didn't have to work?

LF: Yes, I do earn an income with my art. I would love to do ONLY artistic things, and certainly would do it full time if I could.

WF: Has your creative skill improved your life? If so, how?

LF: I've long since discovered that we as humans need art in our lives and in our souls. Most may not realize how much they like and depend on art -- whether it's listening to a favorite radio station, admiring a piece of public art while driving by, selecting comfort colors in clothing, even while doodling on a piece of paper at work.

Art feeds our souls, and without it, our lives would be boring indeed.

WF: My premise is that 'making art' uses right-brain resources, which strengthens creativity and creative thought, which in turn improves issue resolution and problem solving. Give one example in which you've had to overcome a personal or family challenge that has forced you to think outside of the box, or outside your comfort zone, to come up with a custom tailored resolution.

LF: A colleague wanted me to run an art gallery and gift shop in a space she had available, while I was running another art gallery with studio spaces, art classes and more. I couldn't imagine doing both, but when I shifted the paradigm to where she and her volunteer organization would run the shop and I would provide the art, it all fell into place nicely. Two years later, they doubled their sales from the first year.

Laurie Fagen lives and works in Chandler, Arizona.
Visit www.readlauriefagen.com, www.lauriefagen.com, and www.fagendesigns.com to see examples of her work.

Patricia Hall, Painter

WF: What do you do?

PH: I currently oil paint.

WF: Do you earn an income doing this? If not, would you do this if you didn't have to work?

PH: I have been able to supplement my income through my painting but do not make a living. I could see myself doing my artwork for a high percentage of the time, but feel like I would have to spend a small percentage of time at least on another path just to keep balance in my life and to get me out with people in a different way.

WF: Has your creative skill improved your life? If so, how?

PH: My creative skills have definitely improved my life because it entails working with the right side of the brain and all that that encompasses. Not only is the right side of the brain responsible for creativity, but also for intuition. As a result creative types are usually very intuitive and in touch with all of the senses. This led to my healing work and was responsible for my success there. It is a crossover field.

WF: My premise is that 'making art' uses right-brain resources, which strengthens creativity and creative thought, which in turn improves issue resolution and problem solving. Give one example in which you've had to overcome a personal or family challenge that has forced you to think outside of the box, or outside your comfort zone, to come up with a custom tailored resolution.

PH: Right-brain people are creative in many ways with art being one of them. Obviously this would entail all of the arts, music, poetry, writing, etc.

I feel problem resolution is definitely something that creative people excel at because they are used to combining "pieces" to create a "whole". Whereas left-brain people also have the skill to problem solve, they can be limited by their determination and proclivity to adhere to what is "logical". As a result they miss out on new possibilities that right-brain people often bring forth. However, the caveat is...people with too much right-brain influence often lack the ability to make their ideas manifest. The result is the artist who dreams too much and lacks the ability to produce or make manifest their dreams. So to really create, there has to be a delicate balance of both sides of the brain working.

I have always been creative. I worked with fiber arts for 25 years professionally, utilizing appliqué and embroidery to create wearable art. I gave it up about 12 years ago and stopped doing anything in the way of the traditional creative arts. That began an intense journey of self-discovery and a dive into the world of the healing arts...a different but related art form. Among other modalities, I studied a type of regression therapy that worked with deep trauma. Needless to say, it unleashed many things that had long been hidden in Pandora's Box...things that left behind an intense feeling of anger.

Through a meditation one day, I was given the advice of a Samurai who told me that it was painting that had always helped me keep my balance and that if I didn't paint, I soon fell out of balance. He asked me to remember that the Samurai was bound to not only master his warrior skills, but, as a balance of forces, was obliged to master his choice of arts. It didn't take long to realize his sage advice was right on the mark. It made sense.

Since that time, I have been able to use that ancient wisdom of the Samurai and with direct purpose have sought balance between the two brains, between the emotions and between the spirit by actively pursuing oil painting as a way to balance the intense energies that are a part of my being.

Jacque Lynn Keller, Acrylic Painter & Designer

WF: What do you do?

JK: I am a visual, freelance and fine artist. I enjoy acrylic painting, logo design, site-specific work and design.

WF: Do you earn an income doing this? If not, would you do this if you didn't have to work?

JK: Yes…on both counts.

WF: Has your creative skill improved your life? If so, how?

JK: The process of painting and creating is like my own form of meditation…it keeps me in tune with my own abilities and imagination. There is a favorite quote "Earth without Art is just Eh!"

WF: My premise is that 'making art' uses right-brain resources, which strengthens creativity and creative thought, which in turn improves issue resolution and problem solving. Give one example in which you've had to overcome a personal or family challenge that has forced you to think outside of the box, or outside your comfort zone, to come up with a custom tailored resolution.

JK: I believe that using my creative side helps in every aspect of my life: dealing with my children, family, friends, and every stranger I meet. Creating makes me a happier person therefore I give more of my best self to those whose lives I touch.

Jacque L. Keller lives with her family in Arizona. She, along with John Gleason, is a co-owner of Quant'm Art Inc. and you can see her artwork and designs at

www.QuantumArtInc.com, or reach her at
info@QuantumArtInc.com.

Dale Kesel, Photographer

WF: What do you do?

DK: I am a professional photographer with 21 years of experience creating images that move people emotionally. I apply the discipline of creating emotionally engaging images in my fine art photography as well as my commercial and portrait work. I teach the principles of design, composition and lighting through private classes in which the camera is our primary tool. I also lead field trips into the most picturesque areas of the Southwest to give hobbyists and aspiring professional photographers exposure to wonderful subject matter from the mountains to the lakes, streams and magnificent land formations that are abundant throughout our region of the U.S.

WF: Do you earn an income doing this? If not, would you do this if you didn't have to work?

DK: Since I moved to Arizona in 1991, Photography has been my profession, and therefore, my means of making a living and providing for my family. Photography has always been a part of my life. I grew up as the person in our family who documented all of our special occasions, vacations, etc. I continued to use photography as a creative outlet during my 20-year advertising career from 1971 to 1991. I have an extreme passion for expressing myself through photography. And, yes, it would be a big part of my life, even if I did not have to work.

WF: Has your creative skill improved your life? If so, how?

DK: My creative skill, as it has developed over my lifetime, has definitely made my life richer. The more I shoot with my camera, the more I see in every waking moment.

With every photographic assignment and every trip into the field with my camera, I learn, my awareness and sensitivity increases and I am able to create increasingly compelling and meaningful images for clients and for people who have a passion for art.

WF: My premise is that 'making art' uses right-brain resources, which strengthens creativity and creative thought, which in turn improves issue resolution and problem solving. Give one example in which you've had to overcome a personal or family challenge that has forced you to think outside of the box, or outside your comfort zone, to come up with a custom tailored resolution.

DK: In 2001, following the 9/11 World Trade Center disaster, I was forced to close my Photography Studio, which I had operated for eleven years. Instead of changing careers, I pursued my passion for creating powerful and compelling images with my camera, using my home as my office and my studio. At this time, I expanded my photographic work into teaching photography at the college level and privately. I also began to lead private photography field trips and seminars that took me to many places which I never had the time to visit when I owned the studio. Instead of a disaster, this experience was very freeing. It broadened my creative experience and lead me to share what I had gained from my photography career with hundreds of other people who were hungry to learn more.

Seeing others dramatically increase their photographic abilities has been very rewarding. Today, I look at what I do as a means of sharing with others what was so freely given to me.

Dale Kesel resides in Phoenix, AZ. You can see many of his photographs and learn more about his photography at www.keselimages.com or www.keselphotography.com, or email him dkesel@keselimages.com.

Debbie Kyle, Crochet & Knit Designer

WF: What do you do?

DK: I design, create and sell crochet and knit items through my Internet business, HandmadeBabyLove.com. My products mostly consist of beautifully crafted baby gifts and newborn photography props.

WF: Do you earn an income doing this? If not, would you do this if you didn't have to work?

DK: I do earn an income doing this, and I love it. I think part of what keeps me at it is that regardless of what income comes in, I'm always designing and creating. I love my work, and if I couldn't make money at it, it would still be a part of my life as something to do in my free time.

WF: Has your creative skill improved your life? If so, how?

DK: I believe it has. It gives me an outlet for stress and frustration. I work out a lot of issues with my knitting needles. I also find it very gratifying to physically make something with my own hands - to come up with an idea, and see it manifest right before me.

WF: My premise is that 'making art' uses right-brain resources, which strengthens creativity and creative thought, which in turn improves issue resolution and problem solving. Give one example in which you've had to overcome a personal or family challenge that has forced you to think outside of the box, or outside your comfort zone, to come up with a custom tailored resolution.

DK: Well... I actually deal with living outside my comfort zone on a daily basis.

Living off of self-employment income is not always easy, and I'm always coming up with ways to make a dollar stretch further. Not only am I a business owner, but I'm also a single parent, and coming up with creative ways to make sure my son has everything he needs is a daily creative exercise. He's come to know the joys of card games over a trip out for pizza, and how dancing around the living room to songs playing on the computer can be just as fun as going out to the movies. What he doesn't realize is how much money we're saving. As I struggle to come up with fun activities and tasty homemade meals, my creative side gets a work out!

Debbie Kyle lives with her son, and designs and creates for her Internet business, Handmade Baby Love, in Chandler, AZ. To see her unique designs and hand created baby wear or to send her an email, visit http://handmadebabylove.com.

Bob Leighton, Photographer

WF: What do you do?

BL: I've always been intrigued by the idea of capturing beautiful images with a photograph. In my late teens, I acquired a Nikon SLR camera. As I recall, it was an F2 with a pure black body. I loved this camera. I'd shoot macro photos of flowers, fowl on the pond, people, landscapes, etc. Boxes and boxes of developed images were plentiful.

Then on a visit to Mexico I had an accident involving my camera and a bottle of wine in the same satchel. I quickly learned that white wine and an F2 are not good companions and I was minus one Nikon. While I acquired another Nikon, unfortunately it wasn't an F2. And while I took many shots of family and friends over the ensuing years, the passion faded a bit. Then digital came of age. I purchased many early digital cameras and was never satisfied with the quality of the image.

In 2006, I relocated to central Pennsylvania not far from Amish country. The landscapes are majestic as are the sunrises and sunsets. I had to have a camera and shortly thereafter acquired a D200 digital SLR. My passion was reignited. Since then I've taken thousands of photographs, with the sole intent of capturing an image. With the advent of social media, I've had the pleasure of sharing images with friends via Facebook, Shutterfly and Twitter. It gives me great joy to see others react to something that I captured in a brief moment in time … like a sunset, or a moon rising over the lake or even a hummingbird.

WF: Do you earn an income doing this?

BL: I presently don't earn an income via photography, but I have given it consideration. If I didn't need to have another full-time career, and finances were no issue, I could certainly spend my life traveling the world capturing beautiful images.

WF: Has your creative skill improved your life?

BL: My photography has absolutely brought great joy and pleasure to my life. I remember years ago, I captured a picture of my wife's grandfather in a candid photo. I captured his "essence" in a single shot. The photograph was reproduced and shared with all family members. It was and will forever be the photo that captured "Bob Thompson" one of those people for whom the mold was broken after his arrival; a true "salt of the earth." As I recollect, he was probably watching a Red Sox game when I took the shot. This type of photo opportunity has been repeated often through the years.

WF: My premise is that 'making art' uses right-brain resources, which strengthens creativity and creative thought, which in turn improves issue resolution and problem solving. Give one example in which you've had to overcome a personal or family challenge that has forced you to think outside of the box, or outside your comfort zone, to come up with a custom tailored resolution.

BL: In relocating to Pennsylvania in 2006, I was offered an opportunity to become the president of a company with approximately five hundred employees and associates. While I thoroughly enjoyed this leadership role, my time in Pennsylvania ended in mid 2010. For the first time in my business career, I found myself in a very odd place ... unemployed. In reflection, I believe one of those things that helped me to remain focused at an incredibly challenging time was my "art" ... my photography. Late in 2010, I attended two Nikon photography courses to endeavor to improve my skill.

During this time period I considered publishing a book of photographs, and considered photography as my work. While I opted not to go in that direction, I believe my camera and looking through the lens on a regular basis was one of those things that provided perspective and focus. After thirteen months of being unemployed, I was recruited to a great company ... but I've vowed never to put my camera down for the rest of my days. It is my "art."

Bob Leighton is a Real Estate professional and photographer, and resides with his family in Connecticut. He can be reached via email at rwljr57@gmail.com.

Jacqueline Price, Painter

WF: What do you do?

JP: I paint seascapes, landscapes, and still life paintings on canvas or board in acrylics. I also draw but that is for fun and to improve my skills as an artist overall.

WF: Do you earn an income doing this? If not, would you do this if you didn't have to work?

JP: Not currently although that is my ultimate goal. However, because my husband is employed I do have the luxury to paint full-time whether it makes money or not. If I did need to be employed outside of art, I would still make art in my spare time.

WF: Has your creative skill improved your life? If so, how?

JP: Painting and drawing provides a creative outlet that feeds my soul really deep down more than other creative activities I have tried. I feel more complete. It just doesn't feel right to not do it. Also, the colors I use in my paintings have a very physical effect on me. The bright colors I use bring joy to my senses.

WF: My premise is that 'making art' uses right-brain resources, which strengthens creativity and creative thought, which in turn improves issue resolution and problem solving. Give one example in which you've had to overcome a personal or family challenge that has forced you to think outside of the box, or outside your comfort zone, to come up with a custom tailored resolution.

JP: In my immediate family there is a history of mental illness. My mother suffered from depression and several phobias and sometimes threatened suicide although she eventually died from a smoking-related disease. Five years ago, my brother committed suicide at the age of 52. I grew up in an atmosphere of negativity and fear of life, which is something I have had to battle against ever since.

I wanted to be an artist at seven years old but was strongly discouraged and told I couldn't draw. When I did begin to make art, this background of negativity began to haunt and hinder me. Although I made some progress, it was slow and spasmodic. Part of the reason for this was because in art you progress through trial and error. However, when growing up my mistakes were treated as character flaws, so making art could also be a means of dragging me down.

This situation of my need to make art coupled with the distress doing so could produce could not continue. I either had to give up making art or give up the distress. I decided to give up the later. To do so I have had, for the first time in my life, to view problems, errors or 'mistakes' as the opportunity to learn and improve or overcome a barrier, rather than a statement on the quality of my character or worth. As a result, rather than being a stick to beat myself with, art is becoming (this is an on-going process) the means for me to develop skills that can flow across to other parts of my life.

Particularly since my brother's suicide, art has often been a bright, colorful light keeping away the darkness waiting in the wings threatening to envelope me.

Born in England, Jacqueline lives with her husband and paints in Southern California. Her artwork can be seen at www.JacquelineFineArt.com, and writing at http://artbeachlife.blogspot.com.

Sandra Neumann Wilderman, Painter

WF: What do you do?

SNW: I am a full-time artist and paint primarily in watercolor. I also work in acrylic and mixed media. My approach to painting is to pour layers of watercolor or acrylic onto wet paper or canvas creating biomorphic shapes and linear sharpness. After 9/11 I began experimenting with various techniques, formats and compositions and developed the symbolic paintings. More recently, I pour and paint directly on the paper and then weave two paintings together to create a systematic, geometric and textural composition. After painting directly for more than twenty years, I find the spontaneity, the fluidity and the stylistic eclecticism of pouring paint to be a freeing and spiritual experience. And it is through this process that I have found my voice. I also teach watercolor classes and private lessons.

WF: Do you earn an income doing this? If not, would you do this if you didn't have to work?

SNW: I earn an income doing this, but not enough to support myself. And if I did not have to work I would still want to paint and teach art.

WF: Has your creative skill improved your life? If so, how?

SNW: Painting has improved my life in several ways. It is a creative outlet for me, it calms me when I am stressed, and I am more confident and more out-going. I am much more aware of my surroundings and I am comfortable expressing myself through my art. When I look at something, I do not see the object, or a landscape, but instead I see shapes, light and shadows.

Teaching art has improved my life by making me think about how I paint and why I paint the way I do. I started teaching because people wanted to know how I painted with watercolor. And I find it to be a rewarding way to supplement my income. I love seeing people get excited about creating art and painting with watercolors.

WF: My premise is that 'making art' uses right-brain resources, which strengthens creativity and creative thought, which in turn improves issue resolution and problem solving. Give one example in which you've had to overcome a personal or family challenge that has forced you to think outside of the box, or outside your comfort zone, to come up with a custom tailored resolution.

SNW: One of my biggest personal losses is the death of my parents. In 2009, my Father passed away with complications from Alzheimer's and exactly three years and one day later, May 6, 2012, my Mother passed away after having two strokes and in the last year, she was also diagnosed with Alzheimer's. I want to honor my parents and deal with all the emotions I am feeling by creating a series of portraits of each member of my biological family, in an expressionistic rather than representational style.

Sandra Neumann Wilderman lives with her husband in Gilbert, AZ. Her artwork can be seen at http://sandra-neumann-wilderman.fineartamerica.com.

Appendix A: Play and Learn Exercises

Play & Learn: Remembering Joy   13

Play & Learn: ME Diagrams   15

Play & Learn: How Happy Are You?   29

Play & Learn: Finding Your Beginning   35

Play & Learn: Thinking from Your Right-brain   45

Play & Learn: Finding Strength   52

Play & Learn: Meditation   56

Play & Learn: Affirmations   57

Play & Learn: Finding Positive Support   59

Play & Learn: Finding Faith, Hope and Trust   68

Play & Learn: Finding ME Time   76

Play and Learn: Who Are You?   90

Play & Learn: Your Life Mission Statement & Plan   99

Play & Learn: Finding Motivation   102

Play & Learn: Organizing Your Space   105

Play & Learn: Seeking Income   109

Play & Learn: Who is Your Audience or Market?   111

Play & Learn: Art in Your Community   119

Play & Learn: Giving Back   121

Play & Learn: ME Diagrams #2   130

Appendix B: Resources & Suggested Reading

The Art Spirit. Robert Henri, Boulder, CO: Westview Press, ICON Edition: 1984.

The Artist's Way, A Spiritual Path to Higher Creativity. Julia Cameron, New York, NY: G.P. Putnam's Sons, 1992.

The Experience of Place. Tony Hiss, NY, NY: Vintage Books, a division of Random House, Inc. 1990.

Change Your Thoughts, Change Your Life. Dr. Wayne Dyer, CA & NY: Hay House, 2007.

Drawing on the Right Side of the Brain, Betty Edwards. Jeremy P. Tarcher/Putnam, a member of Penguin Putnam, Inc. 1999.

Getting in the Gap, Dr. Wayne Dyer, CA & NY: Hay House, 2003.

Harold and the Purple Crayon. Crocket Johnson, Harper Collins Publishers, 1952.

Manifest Your Destiny – The Nine Spiritual Principles for Getting Everything You Want. Dr. Wayne Dyer, New York, NY: HarperCollins Publishers, 1997.

Pathways to Bliss, Mythology and Personal Transformation. Joseph Campbell. New World Library; 1ST edition, 2004.

The Power of Positive Thinking. Norman Vincent Peale, New York, NY: Fireside, a division of Simon & Schuster, Inc. 2003.

The Rise of the Creative Class. Richard Florida, New York, NY: Basic Books, a member of the Perseus Books Group, 2002.

The Wish-Tree. John Ciardi, Crowell-Collier Press, 1962.

Zen Seeing, Zen Drawing – Meditation in Action. Frederick Franck, New York, NY: Bantam Books, 1993.

About the Author

Wendy Fallon is a professional writer and artist residing in Phoenix, Arizona with her husband. She studied Fine Art at the University of Connecticut and Architecture at the Catholic University of America in Washington, DC. For the last 20 years she has worked as a technical and content writer, a graphic and fine artist, and as both a freelancer and a corporate employee.

You can see samples of her art and writing at
www.wendyfallon.com